# "IT HAPPENED TO ME!"

say people who have lived through strange and unexplainable adventures in the Bermuda Triangle. Adi-Kent Thomas Jeffrey, specialist in the mysteries of this intriguing area, has tracked down those lucky survivors. In this book, she names names and quotes the words of those fortunate enough to return—people such as:

- Bob de la Parra whose sloop was **run down** by a phantom tanker.
- Lloyd and Jean Wingfield who witnessed a most peculiar, soundless, odorless fire at sea.
- Francis Wagner who had several brushes with death and was saved by mysterious advance "messages."

Read about them and the others who came closest to disappearing. Unlike their luckless fellow-adventurers, they **can** tell you what happened when **THEY DARED THE DEVIL'S TRIANGLE.**

Books by Adi-Kent Thomas Jeffrey

*They Dared The Devil's Triangle*
*Triangle of Terror And Other Eerie Areas*
*The Bermuda Triangle*

Published by
**WARNER BOOKS**

# They Dared The Devil's Triangle

by
Adi-Kent Thomas Jeffrey

WARNER BOOKS

A Warner Communications Company

WARNER BOOKS EDITION
First Printing: November, 1975

Cover design by Gene Light

Warner Books, Inc., 75 Rockefeller Plaza, New York, N. Y. 10019

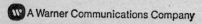 A Warner Communications Company

Printed in the United States of America

Not associated with Warner Press, Inc. of Anderson, Indiana

To Gil and Lynda—my shipmates on many
a wondrous voyage!

# Contents

# Introduction

Earth has many mind-defying puzzles but none more baffling than that mysterious area of Atlantic Ocean lying off the southeast coast of the United States where craft and men have been disappearing without a trace for centuries . . . an area known as "The Bermuda Triangle" or "The Devil's Triangle."

Reams of words have been written about the curious enigma over the past few years, my own book, *The Bermuda Triangle*, being one of the earliest investigations into the subject. More recently, my latest examination into a further possible Triangle zone in the Indian Ocean appeared under the title, *Triangle of Terror and Other Eerie Areas.*

Now with the publication of this present collection of true tales the curiosity goes on as it always will, I am certain. These stories concern not just the vanished ones, which grip our attention with their awe and unresolved mystery, but tell also of a new side to the terror—that experienced by people who traveled into the Triangle *and came back to tell about it!* Their accounts raise the hair strands from the scalp as we empathize with these people. Now we can hear first-hand, in many instances, of exactly what kinds of things, feelings, and events can take place when one travels into the Triangle.

When we enter into this strange world with them, let us lift our faces to the winds of mystery and not cover our senses with the impenetrable armor of suspicion and skepticism so that we cannot feel the delicious terror of the Unknown or hear the voices of the troubled. Let us not don the thick helmet of closed-mindedness under the guise of so-called "common sense" or "reason." This scholarly defense equipment for man's mind is designed to rebuff anything that cannot be understood.

Fortunately, phenomena are too elusive and too stubborn when they do make a showing to be shunted aside just like that! The Unexplained survives through all ridicule, all scorn, all cries of "Claptrap!" from the narrow-minded. Such intellectual butchery as that which has been practiced recently in attempts to debunk the Triangle problem can no more kill off the Mystery Zone than it could, after centuries of trying, eliminate the Loch Ness Monster or the Abominable Snowman. Both those creatures are alive and well and flourishing nicely, as evidenced by recent scientific acceptance and investigation.

Will it take centuries for the Triangle puzzle to undergo serious examination? Let us hope not.

# Chapter 1

## THE CHALLENGERS

The region of the deadly Triangle can be visualized, as almost everyone knows by now, in the form of a very crude triangle. Considering Bermuda as the apex of the triangle and Norfolk, Virginia, as one base angle and Puerto Rico as the other base angle, one can get a rough concept of that zone which has come to be known as "The Bermuda Triangle" or "The Devil's Triangle."

The mystery of what happened to the craft that vanished here and to their occupants has become one of the prime puzzles of our time. Although disappearances have occurred in waters all over the world, none have happened with such alarming regularity and concentration as in the Triangle zone and none with such complete, utter "disintegration." Never a clue is forthcoming.

Usually the pattern with all of the vanished craft is similar. The weather at the time was average to good—oftentimes excellent. There was seldom a hint of trouble with the ship or plane—no SOS sent. Then the final bafflement: no debris or remnant of sail or clothing or craft. Nothing.

What is going on in the Devil's Triangle?

Speculations abound. Some I covered in my book, *The Bermuda Triangle.* Some I cover in the closing chapters of this book. But they still all stand as speculations. There is no final answer yet.

If a New Jersey yachtsman has his way, however, there will be explanations soon. He intends to find out for himself what key will unlock the solution to the Devil's Triangle mystery. He makes a dedicated point of sailing into the deadly zone as frequently as he can manage it.

Is Robert de la Parra asking for trouble?

The answer is "Yes!"

But the calm assurance in the steady voice of this wavy-haired, dark-bearded, 34-year-old, and much-experienced sailor tells you he knows what he is talking about and always knows what he's doing.

Bob de la Parra brings skill and an analytical mind to his task. He is an engineer and a portrait artist. He is also an excellent amateur yachtsman.

In an interview recently with a *Philadelphia Bulletin* reporter, Francis T. Geary, de la Parra said, "I keep mulling the whole fantastic Triangle problem over and over in my mind. It gets in your blood, you know. I'm aware sailing the Triangle is a challenge, but I can't put it aside. You go in and you come out. But it doesn't end there. You have to keep at it. It becomes a compulsion.

"I have a theory, and I'd like to personally find out if I'm right. Of course, I'd like to live to tell about it, too!"

To explain his theory, de la Parra picked up a globe model of the earth, then laid out maps illustrating the topography of the floors of the Atlantic and Pacific Oceans.

"You'll notice," the engineer pointed out to the reporter, "that the Bermuda or Devil's Triangle covers the deepest trenches that exist on the bottom of the Atlantic. And in the Japan area where we have a Triangle counterpart called the 'Devil's Sea,' the waters cover the deepest trenches known in the Pacific Ocean—although the disappearances in the Japanese area have not been as intense as in the Atlantic zone.

"Now I am convinced that at various times there is an associated, but not directly related, cascading current force within these trenches which causes an extensive reaction on the water surface, much the same as a spilling effect when a stop is pulled from a bathtub."

Robert de la Parra paused to light a pipe, then continued, "This surface reaction is by no means limited. It covers miles, pirouetting gradually like an increasingly deepening canyon toward the vortex where ships and aircraft alike are sucked down in the world's largest vacuum!"

When asked about how this could affect aircraft such as the famous case of the five vanished Avenger bombers in 1945, the artist-engineer replied:

13

"I believe all those planes, whose pilots were governed by altimeters, simply flew lower and lower into the massive canyon of the vortex, sucked down to great depths and crushed to bits and pieces by the tremendous subterranean pressures.

"Having flown lower when monitoring the altimeters," de la Parra continued, "the pilots reported what they saw from deep inside the vortex. Naturally, the instruments went haywire. The planes were now below sea level. The sun, instead of being overhead, was out on the distant horizon, if visible at all."

Robert de la Parra has this interesting personal viewpoint and he is dedicating his "cruise time" to trying to prove it. The whole world will be waiting for the results.

Has he ever experienced any Triangle weirdness to date on these investigative trips, I asked.

Robert de la Parra was not long in answering me.

"One of the strangest and most inexplicable things that ever occurred to me.

"In April of 1972 two friends of mine, Bill Heinly and John DeCou, and I went for a sail off South Port, North Carolina, in Heinly's 36-foot sloop, *Spielkamrad*. We set out at dawn and cut through the reef at Cape Fear, then set a course to pass Cape Lookout (the same course taken by the 'ghost ship,' the *Carroll A. Deering,* in 1921!). We planned to round Cape Hatteras by way of Diamond Shoals.

"Well, the weather was clear that day and night, and we passed Cape Lookout in good weather and good spirits. As we approached Diamond Shoals, I

14

made the decision to head out to sea. We left the shoreline behind and put our port parallel to Diamond Shoal, although the night was falling and the light from Diamond Shoal could not be seen.

"We were out no more than a few hours when Bill Heinly decided to sack out, leaving John and me to tend *Spielkamrad*. The weather was getting dirty, but nothing we couldn't handle.

"After a short time I noticed in the distance what appeared to be a large tanker. This was not an uncommon sight in this part of the ocean, for we were in the heart of the shipping lanes.

"I set out to do what I had done, in just such a situation, many times before—I set a course with what seemed to be the tanker's intended course, so as to intersect when close enough to determine the tanker's true course, falling off so as not to interfere with its heading.

"I reasoned that in this case, the likelihood of *Spielkamrad* intersecting with the tanker was quite remote—the tanker was too far off in the distance and we were making poor headway, as the rough seas were setting us back.

"But, within minutes, the tanker was on us, bearing down like the large black shadow of a shark! Its port and starboard lights gleamed at us like a monster's one red and one green eye! I had miscalculated severely both our speed and the tanker's course!

"John and I watched in horror with the realization that this huge tanker—utterly silent and without a name—was about to cut little *Spielkamrad* in half!

"We sprang into action fighting with the sails and

15

the helm to bring the ship about in a vain effort to avoid collision, shouting for Bill as we did so. It's hard to explain my thoughts at that moment. It seemed to me Time and Space were frozen and yet speeding ahead in unison . . .

"I thought Bill would never reach the deck. My bones seemed to contract within me as I braced for the shock of collision. I could almost feel the bow of the tanker slicing at our midsection—

"At that instant Bill reached us, asking curiously what the danger was. Almost in unison John and I replied by pointing to the dark shadow of death on top of us, but to our amazement only the *stern* of a large-hulled tanker was visible—on our other side! It was disappearing quietly and quickly, leaving us behind it, undisturbed and dead in the water. John and I couldn't believe what we saw! The vessel was slipping rapidly away from us without any noise or wake or even, we noticed, any smell of smoke from its stacks!

"Both John and I can swear to you we saw what we saw and that there was no way that tanker could have gotten where it got to without passing through us. The chill of that night rekindles itself in me every time I think about it. Where else but in the Devil's Triangle could such a thing have occurred?"

With that question, I wondered whether or not Bob de la Parra would, indeed, continue to invade the haunting Triangle, seeking an answer.

He assured me he would.

He is not alone in this compulsion to get to the bottom of the puzzling problem. Every day more and more investigators like Robert de la Parra are challenging the Triangle dangers to come up with some final solution.

Two such daring-doers are right now, as of this writing, planning their respective challenges from the far West.

One is a veteran captain of the sea, Jim Nash of Wilmington, California. He wrote me recently of his forthcoming expedition into the Devil's Triangle, inviting me to join him and a crew of 16 researchers who intend to probe, to the greatest possible degree, the mystery of this area.

Captain Nash is outlining a "research and exploratory expedition into the Bermuda Triangle aboard a 100-foot vessel with the serious intent and desire to perform as scientific an exploration as possible into this strange phenomenon."

Cheers and salutations to Captain Nash! Were I not off shortly on another farther-afield expedition, I would be with him!

From Ogden, Utah, comes another letter from a serious researcher. J. L. Hawkins tells me:

"Someone should go into the Bermuda Triangle area and attempt—I stress the word 'attempt'—to discover what is creating such a strange phenomenon.

"My friends and I have discussed this innumerable times. We are well aware of the dangers involved for the person that would be undertaking this voyage . . . Being the only person that is neither married nor attached to anyone now, or in the foreseeable future, it was decided that I and, possibly, one other would attempt this undertaking. We will try to discover what is happening in this ill-famed area . . ."

17

To me, the greatest virtue of any phenomenon is its inherent ability to bring out the noblest and the bravest in the men who examine it.

Best of good wishes, challengers all!

# Chapter 2

## THINGS THAT GO SPLASH
## IN THE NIGHT

Divers who have spent much of their lives exploring the fascinating and near-bottomless waters of the Caribbean all speak of this region in awed tones. To their ilk, this is man's last frontier. These courageous men who plumb the lime-hued depths are risking their lives for the thrill of standing where no man has ever stood before to look upon a world never seen by such as they before.

The famous—or perhaps more rightly called, infamous—Blue Holes of the Bahamas have challenged man's curiosity for many long years. The natives roll their eyes at the very mention of these deadly caverns.

"You go down dere," any one of them will tell you, "an' you never seen again. De Lucsa, him of de hands, he pull you into de lair . . . and you gone down dere *forever*!"

For centuries the natives of the Bahamas have told tales of the terrible monsters and devils that make their homes beneath the sea. It is because of their deadly whims that ships and men have been disappearing over the ages. The creatures have dragged them into their watery caves and consumed them . . .

The July 1973 issue of *Saga* magazine printed an article by Charles Gnaegy on the "Deadly Mystery of the Bahama Blue Holes." In it the author described the awesome adventures of scuba diver Bob Wallace and his team in the waters just off Eleuthra in the eastern Bahamas.

All of the crew felt the thrill of investigation in an untrodden world . . . a world so dark that fellow creatures down there had never seen each other until the light of these men brought vision to their eternal night.

Gnaegy gives the fascinating background history of this underwater universe:

"Geological history states that the Bahama Islands, 1000-mile-long string of emerald green dots in the Atlantic Ocean off Southern Florida, were formed about 130 million years ago as banks of limestone rising from the ocean floor. When the last great Ice Age froze most of the earth's surface, water levels lowered considerably and the Bahama banks were exposed. Then, as the surface began to thaw, trickles of water seeped into the limestone, refroze, thawed, and began to form sinkholes and eventually caverns. When the full thaw came, the oceans rose hundreds of feet, leaving the caves submerged and closed off to man—until recently."

Bob Wallace was one of the first to attempt to explore these caverns that wind in such intricate labyrinths no one has ever, as yet, found his way to their end.

Many divers, over the years, have vanished in these depths, and even more incredibly, boats have been drawn into these mysterious holes to disappear forever! Are these incidents all related to whirlpool action, tides, age-old sinkholes? Or are there deeper mysteries to be probed?

Most underwater divers I spoke to felt that there were. The tales brought back by these men, I found, bore a marked similarity to each other.

Typical are the comments given me by Louis Lento of Hollywood, Florida:

"Believe me, I have seen a lot of strange things in the Bermuda Triangle! Especially in the '50s and '60s. Not only weird lights, but dark forms on moonless nights. Though on such occasions it would be too dark to make out a firm outline, I could see vague shapes—dark and solid-looking, though indeterminate of design.

"Sometimes they seemed to be descending into the water—I could hear the splash as they plunged in. At other times, they appeared to be emerging *out* of the water. I can't describe to you exactly what they looked like, it was always so dark (and nothing is so dark as the ocean when there's no light source from anywhere), but one thing I can tell you for sure: they weren't sharks, dolphins, barracudas, or fish of any kind. Neither were they whales. These forms were far too large to be any species of fish or mammal."

Another man who has devoted most of his adult life to skin diving is Andie Gorman of New Hope,

Pennsylvania. In fact, for him, diving is more profession than spare-time pleasure. He works frequently with such problem-probers as the U.S. Navy at Annapolis, where he aided in examining mini-sub ailments.

Andie, too, has spotted his share of strange forms and eerie lights beneath the surface of the Triangle waters.

"One thing I know: there's got to be something out there . . . I've seen 'em too often! What such things are, we can't say yet, but I'm betting on it that we will someday soon!"

The experience of a Coastguardsman I interviewed certainly lends credence to the theory that something strange occurs in the ocean depths in the Triangle Zone. His story, which I cover in Chapter 16, tells of the strange experience of his ship receiving over and over a Mayday message on the emergency frequency which, when tracked down, always vanished. The moment the ship returned to its "station," the message would come again, "Mayday! Mayday!"

"We never did locate the distressed vessel or whatever it was," the young man told me.

Commercial fishermen off the southern coast of the U.S. report from time to time witnessing freakish goings-on in this Twilight Zone of the Atlantic. One such account came from a fishing vessel trawling in lower Biscayne Bay in the middle of the night. Suddenly its compass veered from pointing north to the direction of west. This was startling to the men. There was no hint of storm or atmospheric disturbance of any kind. The night was serene, the seas calm as bath water.

The men decided to check their position in rela-

22

tion to the light on the power company's water tower off their port side. They then ascertained that they had not moved; only the compass had switched directions!

In the seconds following, a startling thing occurred: beneath the bright moonlight, distinctly visible, a huge black object hovered close to the shoreline ahead of them! The thing remained stationary without making a sound for several minutes; then swiftly it dropped from sight.

As soon as it was gone, the compass returned to normal.

An equally awesome experience occurred to Lloyd Frederick of West Hollywood, California. He was serving on a destroyer, the *U.S.S. Murray*, in 1954, stationed at a gun director, when he observed through the optics the weirdest sight of his life! Through a clear, cloudless sky a large object, pale white and translucent, bore down in the *Murray*'s direction, paused and hovered a few seconds, then was gone!

Frederick swung quickly toward the torpedoman who was observing through the other set of optics alongside. He didn't have to open his mouth.

"Did you see that?" the torpedoman yelped at him.

The two sailors compared notes. They had each seen through two completely separate sets of optics the identical sight.

When pressed for a description, Frederick paused, thought a moment, then with half a smile as though expecting me to gape open-mouthed said:

"Yeah, I'd say it looked most of all like a gigantic jellyfish!"

I did gape, open-mouthed.

So have millions of others who ponder the fantastic and titillating mysteries of the Bermuda Triangle, not a few of which concern the "things that go splash in the night" in this strangest of regions.

# Chapter 3

## GHOSTLY GLOWS
## AND WHEELS OF LIGHT

One phenomenon witnessed more frequently, perhaps, than any other in the Atlantic's Twilight Zone is that of a luminous glow. The presence of glimmering patches or streaks in this area has been reported several times by the astronauts. These radiances are so bright they have been seen from outer space. In fact, the U.S. astronauts state that these shining strips are the last lights visible to them from the earth as they lift skyward.

Columbus, back in 1492, when sailing through these waters witnessed a "remarkable ball of fire" for which he could think of no explanation. Passengers aboard the *Sea Venture,* bearing colonists to the New World in 1609, witnessed a dazzling display of dancing lights in the rigging and along the decks of the vessel late one night.

To this day, lights glimmering off Cape Hatteras in the dead of night are seen from time to time. Since Ocracoke Inlet was the hangout of the pirate Blackbeard (Captain Edward Teach), the sparkling "spook lights" are considered by some oldtimers to be the restless spirits of the pirate crew and are dubbed the "Teach Lights" by the village residents of the Outer Banks. They are seen on occasion both over the waters of Pamlico Sound and within them —or bobbing up and down on the shore.

Are they supernatural lights—or are they signs of an "Other World?"

Most skin divers who have witnessed various glows beneath the surface of the sea feel they tell of Outer Space or Inner Space beings, not spirits of any sort.

Skin diver Louis Lento of Hollywood, Florida, is one underwater man who has seen the phenomena of lights many times. Ten to twenty years ago they were quite common, he tells me. But he still sees them from time to time. They appear suddenly in the darkness of the waters' depths, sometimes as flickers that dazzle for a second, then vanish. Other times the glows stay for quite a while. On one occasion, says Lento, he saw a reddish-white light appear while he was skin diving in the middle of the night. It was so brilliant it lit up the whole area of the water where he was.

Louis Lento has also seen lights above the surface of the water.

"I've seen streaks of brilliance shoot through the air, then disappear into the ocean—all at varying distances. They can make quite a display, I can tell you!"

Aircraft pilots testify also to this phenomenon of

26

eerie lights. One of them is quoted by Charles Berlitz in his book on the Bermuda Triangle. A flyer for a charter plane company in Miami reported experiencing the most fantastic incident of his life on a return trip from Nassau. Just as he was approaching over Bimini he noticed a faint glowing effect on the wings of his plane. Within five minutes the glow became so intense the pilot couldn't read his instruments. Finally the whole cockpit became a glowing area, and the pilot was unable to function. During this time, his instruments all went haywire. After a buildup to a blinding strength, the light began to diminish until finally it faded completely away and all was normal again, including the craft's compasses and directional finder, clocks, etc.

A strange circle of light without any positive explanation for its presence has been picked up on U.S. satellite photos (see Chapter 6).

But the eeriest form such Triangle glows have assumed has been witnessed at least twice in both the Bermuda Triangle and that similar mystery zone, the East Indian Ocean (a region I cover in my book, *Triangle of Terror and Other Eerie Areas*). A gigantic wheel glowed underwater—hub and spokes clearly visible!

The first recorded occasion of such a sighting comes down to us from an old captain's log. The date of entry is June 10, 1909.

The ship in question was a Danish steamer called the *Bintang*. The vessel's course on this strange night took it through the Strait of Malacca which slices between Sumatra and the Malay Peninsula. This region of the East Indian Ocean, according to the calculations of the late Ivan Sanderson, renowned Triangle investigator, scientist and researcher in the Unexplained, constitutes a Far East mystery zone in "line" with Japan's Devil's Sea zone and the Bermuda Triangle. The repetition of the appearance of a giant illumined wheel in both the West Atlantic and the East Indian Ocean regions lends credence to Sanderson's theory.

On that long-ago night in 1909, the *Bintang*'s captain knew nothing of Triangle Zones or mysterious electric forces or possible men from inner or outer space—he knew only that he was seeing the strangest sight ever to pass before him in long years of plying the oceans of the world. His men saw it, as well, and there was no little consternation aboard. The captain described the astonishing event in his log which was later put on record in the files of the Meteorological Institute of Denmark.

The captain was standing on the bridge when his eye was caught by a long luminous line gleaming up from the water. As though it were a giant beam streaming from some great underwater flashlight aimed in their direction, the huge ribbon of light moved slowly across the ship's path. A second later another equally large and glowing band of light arced in front of them. As it moved on, it was followed by another and another.

Suddenly his first mate was at his side.

"What is it, Cap'n?"

There was no answer as the captain shook his head. He continued to stare, transfixed.

After a moment, he wiped perspiration off his brow with one hand. "It appears to be a wheel shaped of light. Look!" The captain pointed straight ahead. In front of them, some distance from the ship, a brilliant spot of light burned in the sea, like a gigantic coal fire in a soot-blackened grate. Out from this heart of light the beams projected, rotating slowly. At the same time the "wheel," the glowing hub with its luminous spokes, revolved closer and closer to the steaming vessel chugging its way through the night. In the words of the log entry itself, "Long arms issued from a center around which the whole system appeared to rotate."

The eerily gleaming wheel revolved closer and closer, without making a sound, toward the *Bintang*. The entire outline of the formation could not be seen at once. It was so huge only half of it appeared from the horizon to the point where the ship coursed its path.

The crew assembled to watch the phenomenon with open-mouthed awe. There was no source from which the lights could issue. It could in no way be a reflection from their own lights, nor was there any other ship in the area at that time.

The captain and his men stared until their eyes ached, straining to catch every movement of the silently rotating disc, gleaming closer and closer. As it came, a strange thing happened. The great wheel began to sink lower and lower into the water's depths as it approached, dimming in its intensity as it sank. Finally it was gone from sight completely and nothing remained to be seen but the black waters of the Strait of Malacca.

The experience had been like a chapter from some Jules Verne novel. Neither the captain nor his men ever ceased talking about the weird incident of that night of June 10th, in 1909.

The Bermuda Triangle displays its mystic wheel also, and one Lewis Van Dercar of Miami can tell you about it.

Van Dercar is a well-known figure in that resort

town of Florida. He is an artist, a psychic, a philosopher, and even a witch. He is also a merchant seaman who knows the seas well.

His experience occurred some years ago when he was sailing about a hundred miles off the coast of Florida. It was a beautiful star-lit night, and he was on deck gazing at the peaceful water with a veteran Norwegian seaman at his side when suddenly a brilliant green glow began to take shape before them from within the dark waters.

Van Dercar and his friend stopped talking and stared. Glowing streamers began to appear from a center of light. "It was like a giant wheel with spokes going out from a central hub," explained Van Dercar later. "I know it sounds screwball and doesn't make sense, but I tell you that's what happened."

The old Norwegian had no trouble accepting the phenomenon. He pointed a gnarled finger in the direction of the glowing wheel.

"See that thing afore, man. In these waters it was, too. And you know something?" He turned toward Van Dercar in the darkness. "It won't do a mite of harm to you 'ceptin' in one way . . ."

Lewis urged him on. "What way?"

"Well," said the old sailor, "it'll drain every bit of strength and energy inside you for a couple days to follow. By the mornin' you'll scarce be able to stir from your bunk!"

"You know something?" Van Dercar will tell you. "The old man was right. Not one of us on board that boat felt able to carry on with the smallest duty the next day. We all felt drained of energy. And we felt that way for several days, too!"

What lies behind the strange phenomenon of the luminous wheel?

Lewis Van Dercar has his own theory. "It's just tied to the whole Bermuda Triangle business. It's one of several places on earth which have strange energy sources. Sounds crazy, but that's what I believe, all the same."

Ruby Yonge, well known as a talk-show host in Miami, has his own theory. He told *Cosmopolitan* magazine in an interview a few years ago, "I'm convinced there's saucer activity in the Triangle, that earth people are collected by the saucer people." He went on to say that he believed two ancient islands remain under the seas in this area—still-intact civilizations with secret reservoirs from which emanate the mysterious patches of glimmering water.

But glows or patches or wheels—whatever form they take, the attention-getting lights from the Triangle zone will apparently be with us for some time to come. They have been with us for centuries in the supernatural world of the mystics. Anyone who has attended a seance has likely seen what the medium calls "spirit lights."

The wheel, also, is not an uncommon phenomenon in ghost lore. Very frequently a "hauntee" reports to me the manifestation of the sound of "wheels grating down a roadway." My own father as a young boy in a Hungarian village at the foot of the Carpathian Mountains used to be awakened from time to time by the rumble of carriage wheels sputtering down the village lanes late at night.

"It's the Black Coach of the Devil coming to our town," his grandmother would tell him, "seeking the souls of the men he has bargained with! He will pick them up and drive them to the edge of earth!"

After such terror, my father seldom found sleep. But he did continue for many years to hear the sound of the coach wheels on various occasions. At such times, when he got the courage to peek out of the casement window, there was never a sign of anything.

So it seems still to be when man tries to get too close to what he sees, it vanishes. Or *he* vanishes!

Which is what the Bermuda Triangle is all about!

# Chapter 4

## UFO'S OVER THE TRIANGLE

In a rural area of Tennessee lives a most unusual man. His name is David Swanner.

David lives, works, and hunts in the remote neck of woods where he has spent all his life. He is happy with his home, his wife, and his two children. He never learned to read or write as schoolchildren do.

But David can recognize the signs of nature. He can read the stars and listen to the tales of the wind. He is closely familiar with the track of the deer, the opossum, and the raccoon. And he knows every bird by its feather and its song.

David Swanner never had the need or the means to roam far afield from all these riches—until a little over two years ago when something occurred, David will tell you, that changed his whole life. On January

17, 1973, the Tennessee woodsman was stalking through a clearing. Suddenly he heard voices.

He paused, lowered his gun, and listened. He heard two people talking. Yet there was no one else around!

He combed the trees and thrashed through the wind-brittled branches, searching. No one.

Presently there was soft laughter. Then silence.

With a shrug, Swanner continued his walking and never mentioned the strange incident to anybody.

Nothing unusual occurred again for many months. Then came a September afternoon when the agile woodsman was out scanning the woods and fields for deer. Something caught his attention—a glow filtered through the forest trees. It seemed to come from a field that stretched on the far side of the wooded area.

Curious, Swanner crunched slowly toward the indefinable object, his footfalls rattling a first sputter of leaves.

When he reached the edge of the woods, his mouth dropped open with amazement. Before him, in the middle of the field, a pearly-glowing round object was just making a descent onto a tripod!

The hunter urged himself closer. He was overcome with curiosity. But when he got within a few feet of the eerie object, somebody or something threw out a shower of a black grainy substance, like heavy pepper. With that, the round glow of light shrank, getting smaller and smaller until finally nothing remained, and David Swanner was alone in the middle of a cotton field staring at empty space.

In that first second of aloneness he heard once again a tiny laugh, then, as before, dead silence.

Today David Swanner, who is far more learned

34

about unidentified flying objects than he was at that astonishing moment two years ago, can tell you what happened that September afternoon. The UFO self-destructed.

He knows many more things now. The glowing object came from a planet that is hidden from our sight by the sun, for it is in the same orbit as earth. The name of the unseen home base is "Planto." It is a twin-planet identical to earth. Its inhabitants are known as "Plantoes."

Two Plantoes visited the field that day in their first contact with David. Until then, he tells you now, they had made their presence known to him only by voice.

Ever since the fall of '73, the two Plantoes have made frequent visits to David Swanner. Their space ship varies in type. Sometimes it is a ball of light; sometimes it is saucer-shaped; sometimes it is in the form of a Dutch wooden shoe. Each ship is surrounded by a glow of light that makes details hard to discern.

But whatever design of craft, the Plantoes have been willing hosts since their first cautious attempts at contact. As a result, David not only has two close friends he never had before, but has traveled far and wide as a guest of the spacemen, all over the globe.

The most fascinating trip for David Swanner, however, was not across the face of the planet; it was just off the southern coast of the United States. It was a space voyage over the Bermuda Triangle! The reason it intrigued the Tennessee woodsman so much was that it was the first occasion on which the two Plantoes did more than transport David through space—they took him through time!

Below him a boat rode the mild waves off the

Florida coast. It was filled with some 200 to 300 passengers, the spacemen advised their guest. But the boat was not below them in 1974; it was a passenger ship cruising down the coastal waters in the year 1948!

David gulped. He was back in time over a quarter of a century!

But that, he soon learned, was not the whole of it. That cruise ship would *itself* transport back in time. Those several hundred people about to leave the big vessel for shore in motor launches would never make the coast. Within minutes, David would see why.

As the space craft darted low, the awed passenger gazed at the sandy shoreline of Florida. Along the beach were clusters of red-skinned natives. They were running into the water screaming and gesturing and throwing an avalanche of sticks and stones at the strange flotilla of loud-chugging craft trying to land.

"It is the year 1735," explained the spacemen to the astonished passenger. "They do not know what to make of the weird boats of wood, metal, and buzzing motors. They are frightened by these men and women in their strange garb, calling out in a tongue they have never heard before."

"As you can see," pointed out one of the Planto men, "the natives of 1735 are not going to let the men of the future—1948—land on their shore!"

The spaceman was right. David could see that. In the next few moments he watched as the Americans hastily withdrew to their cruise ship and re-boarded, obviously in terror.

But that still was not all.

As the space ship zoomed upwards high into the

atmosphere again, David looked back and saw that where the slick luxury liner had been gently riding the waves, there was nothing but an expanse of green ocean.

The second Planto man smiled, his pointy nose quivering ever so slightly. "You are back in 1974, David Swanner. Do not expect you can be seeing that 1948 ship now!"

"Whatever happened to it?" David finally recovered his voice enough to ask.

"It disappeared from off the face of the earth. It went back and back in time. It and the hundreds of people that were on it exist now in another dimension," explained one Planto.

Since that memorable voyage over the Bermuda Triangle, David has been taken into other time dimensions quite often. The Plantoes refer to two sub-dimensions of Time and Space as "The Rear Years" and "The Forward Years."

David Swanner has been taken into both. The people he has met, he could tell you, are unbelievable. For example, he has gone back in time and met Albert Einstein. Now, there are thrilling possibilities ahead in life for David. And the Bermuda Triangle may be a part of that excitement. He may meet Amelia Earhart—or the Plantoes may bring her forward in time to meet David! Surely, she went into another dimension when she vanished in 1937, and it would be easy for the Plantoes to contact her, David feels. What a lot to anticipate!

David Swanner is not the only man to be convinced of these wonders or to have met with the elusive Plantoes. Fellow Tennesseean Stanley Ingram, his good friend and mentor, can tell you the same things. He is a hard-working and sincere individual who has shared these UFO marvels with David. Shared the very cotton field and the very roads where he and David and Stanley's own daughter have come face to face with those most awesome of objects—flying saucers.

Believe the UFO phenomenon or not, one thing is undeniable—countless people describe their sightings. Not a few of them come from the area of the infamous Devil's Triangle.

When one talks to the residents of the coastal stretches of the Triangle, it is common to find people who have seen unidentified flying objects. In fact, I discovered (in Florida and Bermuda particularly) it is a popular form of seaside entertainment to walk along the beach after dark and look for flying saucers. Very few such devotees and curiosity-seekers have been disappointed. Apparently, nearly every night someone sees something.

Saucer-spotting in Florida reached such fruitful proportions a few years ago that one radio station in Miami was able to operate a talk show dedicated entirely to calls and conversation about UFO sightings.

Eyewitnesses come from people in all walks of life—teachers, scientists, newspaper men and women, artists, writers, students, and a great number of pilots and sailors.

Included in that last category as well as in that of writer is Jim Martenoff.

Martenhoff has investigated the Triangle in two capacities. He researched it as a writer (see *Boating* magazine for November 1974) and as a sailor. It was on one such voyage in the mystery zone that Jim was converted from an unbeliever to a believer in UFO's.

It was June of 1968. One of a crew of five, Martenhoff was returning from Dog Rocks about 120 miles southeast of Miami on a 47-foot Sportfisherman called *Rerun*.

About 11:30 in the morning, some 12 miles south-southeast of Islamorada in the Florida Keys, an amazing thing happened that Jim hasn't forgotten to this day. One of the other men joining him on the deck of the flybridge suddenly stared straight ahead and pointed.

"Look!"

Jim lifted his eyes to catch sight of two strange-looking objects swooping gently across their bow, low over the water. They are best described, Jim feels, as inverted bowls, flat on the bottom.

"They were hazy white," Jim says, "very distinct against a clear blue sky. To judge their size and distance was difficult," continues the sailor, "for we had no reference point against which we could compare them.

"But judging by their haziness, they seemed to be quite large and quite far away."

Anyone who suggests to Martenhoff at this point that the two objects might have been conventional aircraft will get a vigorous shake of the head.

"No, they were not regular planes—they were moving too slowly. Also there were no signs of control surfaces or tail assembly. And they were sure not helicopters, as there were no rotors."

But it did seem to Jim the objects might have had tiny, stubby, wing-like projections jutting out from the sides.

The course of these UFO's on that June morning was quick and clear. After crossing the *Rerun*'s bow, the two objects appeared to pick up speed. Soon they were fading in the distance and finally were gone from sight—headed right for the center of the Bermuda Triangle.

Like so many other UFO sighters, Jim Martenhoff doesn't know how to explain what he saw—or whether or not the Saucers have any relation to the Triangle puzzle. All he can tell you is, as thousands of others say; "I saw them."

# Chapter 5

## MAYDAY FROM A USO?

Ufologists generally concur that if Unidentified Flying Objects are zeroing in on earth via the Triangle, then it is equally possible that Unidentified Submersible Objects are having a heyday there also. Such fast-propelled vehicles may be one and the same craft. That is, flying saucers may come from outer space but dive beneath the ocean depths for regenerating power or making contact with landing bases deep within that trench area of the Atlantic.

Or USO's may be ocean-born. Scientist Ivan Sanderson suggested that a whole species of man developed in water and remained underwater where it lives to this day. Are emerging objects from this mystery zone vehicles from such a civilization?

Are such USO's related in any way to a Lost Continent? Some scientists like Manson Valentine, who has devoted a great part of his life to investigating the underwater ruins of ancient civilizations in the Bahamas, believe that indeed they may be.

Whatever the theories, one thing seems apparent: strange things are being seen—and seen frequently—arising out of the watery depths of the Triangle area.

Perhaps such a strange submersible was responsible for the vanishing of the *Witchcraft* at Christmas time in 1967, a story I covered in my book, *The Bermuda Triangle.*

The *Witchcraft,* a 23-foot yacht, was owned by Dan Burrack, owner of a Miami Beach hotel. One night during the holiday season, Burrack invited a visiting friend of his from Fort Lauderdale, Father Patrick Horgan, out for a cruise offshore to enjoy the dazzling skyline of Miami.

One thing is certain, Dan Burrack never gave a thought about safety, for his boat had been called by its builder "absolutely unsinkable" because of built-in flotation chambers. Unfortunately, the builder was proved wrong. Something—or perhaps one should say, some Thing—made the slick yacht vulnerable.

About nine o'clock that night, the Miami Coast Guard received a message from the *Witchcraft.* She had struck some underwater object which although it had not damaged the craft itself, stressed Burrack, had bent the propellors, causing a vibration which worried him. Though the incident wasn't serious and he stated that there was no danger—the boat wasn't taking in water—he felt, nevertheless, they should return to the harbor. Would the Coast Guard give him a tow back to port?

Three minutes later a cutter was on its way. It

was at the designated position within a quarter of an hour, but there wasn't a sign of the *Witchcraft*. They searched thoroughly far out to sea. They tried to raise a response on the radio. They were answered only by silence. No trace of the cabin cruiser was ever discovered.

Nor did they ever uncover the remains of the priest or the hotel owner, or the tiniest particle of any of the flotation equipment—life preservers, life jackets, and air-filled cushions that were on board, or, most unbelievable of all, the slightest remnant of the flotation chambers that were supposed to be unable to sink. They could disappear and did.

Was some unknown submersible responsible?

We will never know.

Two people who may well know more about USO's than anyone else in the baffling Triangle zone are Jean and Lloyd Wingfield of Lighthouse Point, Florida. Lloyd is no poetic dreamer or "way-out" thinker; he is an electronics sales engineer with both feet on the ground—even when he's on board his 22-foot Aquasport and headed for the good fishing depths several miles offshore.

Jean Wingfield, too, is a level-headed Ms who knows whereof she speaks, and she speaks no nonsense. The word of the Wingfields is particularly reliable. When they say such and such happened, you can be sure it did.

The following, one of the strangest, most chilling, stories to come out of the Triangle, occurred to Lloyd and Jean in October of 1973. To this day, they have never forgotten a moment of it.

The couple pulled out from shore on a clear breezy day to a point about seven miles east of Boca Raton. The ocean was gray-blue as they threw their lines over the side and began trawling. It was about two o'clock in the afternoon when Jean first noticed smoke blowing like a ribbon along the horizon.

Thinking little of it, she pulled her hat closer down over her eyes and gazed at the tiny swells of water ahead of her. Nothing was biting yet, but the day was cool and beautiful and filled with the promise of late October's energizing crispness.

Jean turned her gaze to the horizon once more. The streamer of smoke had not moved. It was still winding across the sky at the same point.

"Look, Lloyd," she called over to her husband. "What do you think is causing that smoke? It's been spurting upwards like that without moving for over fifteen minutes."

Lloyd shielded his eyes and stared. "Funny, can't be coming from the stack of a freighter or it'd be moving."

"Nope," agreed Jean. "Sure isn't moving. Coming from the same spot, that's for sure."

"Could be a boat on fire," Lloyd added quickly. "Let's switch the radio to the distress frequency, see what we pick up. Some guys somewhere must be yelling for help."

The Wingfields listened attentively. There wasn't a sign of an SOS coming over the Coast Guard distress channel.

"Isn't that strange," commented Jean. "How far from us do you judge it to be, hon?"

Lloyd squinted. "Oh, I'd say 'bout ten to twelve miles northeast of us." Then he stared thoughtfully around him. "The wind's out of the northeast—you can see it's blowing the smoke southwest—toward Miami."

The husband and wife were silent for a few minutes as they studied the stream of smoke ribboning its way along the horizon just above the water.

With one accord they faced each other, both with the same thought: "Let's push on and see what it is!"

The couple trolled toward it leisurely, yet an obvious curiosity. was taking precedence over any fishing interest. After a short while, they pulled in their lines and picked up speed, for the nearer they got, the more it appeared to be a boat on fire.

Lloyd checked the emergency frequency again. Nothing. Amazing. Hard to understand. Why wasn't somebody Maydaying at that point?

It wasn't until the craft got to within a few hundred yards that the couple realized for the first time that there was no boat on fire—only smoke issuing forth—they couldn't believe it—right out of the ocean itself!

They moved forward closer and closer until they were within a hundred feet of the banner of smoke. What they saw astonished them. A pipe some eight to ten inches in diameter was projecting directly out of the water spewing forth brilliant red flames and belches of yellow smoke!

The Wingfields slowly circled the pipe.

"Good Lord," murmured Lloyd, "look at the angle of the pipe . . . it's gotta be anchored to something under the water—Yet," he continued, looking over at Jean, "How could it be? We're in some 1000 feet of water!"

Jean shook her head, speechless. The two stared without exchanging a word.

"I don't like it," said Jean. "Let's not get any closer."

"Don't worry, hon. Can't figure out what it is, but

I know one thing, we're not going to do any in-depth checking!"

After the boat had completed circling once, Lloyd pulled the power to idle. Quietly the craft bobbed up and down. The Wingfields gazed ahead in awed silence. The pipe appeared to be of a yellowish color. The smoke, too, was saffron-hued, contrasting vividly with the brilliant scarlet of the spewing flames.

"It's positively weird!" pronounced Jean.

"So utterly without sound!" commented Lloyd.

"Or smell!" added Jean.

"Yeah." He glanced over at his wife. "Peculiar, isn't it?"

The two watched without further conversation. Slowly the smoke and flames before them began to diminish. Eventually, they died down completely. Finally, there was nothing left but a stretch of yellowish pipe sticking up ghoulishly from the churning water.

The pipe never moved.

But the Wingfields did. By this time the Gulf Stream had carried them to a point off the coast of Delray Beach about 15 to 18 miles out. They were some hour and a half away from home.

"Let's go back," Jean called into the late afternoon breezes.

"Right, skipper!" replied Lloyd as they chugged quickly back toward home port.

But the day's adventures weren't over yet.

Another unusual thing caught their eye as they headed homeward. A helicopter overhead, as they were about half way between Boca Raton and the Hillsboro Inlet, some three miles out to sea, began to show signs of trouble. Its engine sputtered, fal-

46

tered, and coughed. The pilot brought her down in a quick landing, settling in the softly heaving ocean with a groan.

The Wingfields kept going. They'd had enough of troubled craft.

But just before reaching the Hillsboro Inlet, the couple spied another emergency. A Coast Guard boat was towing a disabled 25-foot cruiser back to port. Just at a point no more than 300 yards off shore, the towed cruiser began to submerge and within seconds was gone from sight!

"Perfectly routine troubles, we're sure, but coming on top of that pipe incident, it was all too much!" declared Jean Wingfield later. A frightening incident with such weird overtones that neither Jean nor Lloyd ever reported the occurrence to the Coast Guard.

"They'd have only laughed at us and thought we were nuts," comments Lloyd.

Which no nuts-and-bolts-thinking Coastguardsman is going to deny. Which, nonetheless, does nothing toward solving the mystery of what happened in the ocean that day in October of 1973.

Perhaps with more stories coming out and more honest investigations going on every day—as there are—we will come to know.

# Chapter 6

## WHAT "HITS" MAN'S WEATHER SATELLITES?

Man's weather probes seemed to burst forth with a bumper crop of inexplicables during the spring of '75.

First off, there were the reports from three Soviet Arctic weather stations, almost simultaneously. They all told of seeing some unidentifiable object hovering in the atmosphere. One station described it as emitting "cone-shaped beams" of light. The witnesses agreed the object was "shining bright."

The second weather station in the Soviet Union sent a transmission at very nearly the same time indicating that men at that base had spotted a "light blue sphere" and it was busy jettisoning, too, but the emission didn't consist of white "cones" of light but a single brilliant red "fireball." The third Soviet

Arctic weather station described seeing a similar object.

In this country, U.S. weather satellites are presenting our scientists with puzzles—but only during their course over the Bermuda Triangle.

In May of '75 a national magazine carried an article on possible weather satellite peculiarities indicating that Locke M. Stuart, Information Specialist at NASA's Goddard Space Flight Center in Greenbelt, Maryland, had revealed a "strange mystery circle" in some of the ESSA 8 weather satellite pictures. The unusual configuration was different from anything he'd ever seen on a satellite picture before, and he'd examined thousands.

A perfect white circle was distinct, positioned directly over the shoreline of Cape Hatteras, North Carolina.

It first occurred to Stuart, according to the article, that there might have been a flaw in his receiving equipment, but he found that the photos of an independent weather station operator exactly tallied with his. And those photos had been received with different equipment!

Reasoning and inquiring further, Stuart found the circle could not be due to sun-glint on a smooth area of water because such a reflection would photograph as an irregular formation, not a perfect circle. Neither could he explain the dark area near the circle, nor the fact that in every other photo of Hatteras taken before or after orbit No. 16,734, the circle wasn't there.

Could this mysterious white circle have a bearing on the phenomena of the Bermuda Triangle? The magazine strongly suggested that it did.

49

But in a recent communication the very interesting Mr. Stuart assured me he is not mystified and never was. He proceeded to explain his findings, making it clear that his comments were his own and not official opinions from NASA nor of the Goddard Space Flight Center.

As physical scientist with the Missions Utilization Office, Locke Stuart's prime concern is interfacing with the user of remotely sensed (satellite and aircraft) images of the earth. While now not directly involved with direct readout from the weather satellites, he did spend a number of years analyzing weather satellite images, mostly for engineering evaluation.

In 1972 a dark circular feature near Pamlico Sound on ESSA 8 was the cause of some discussion between Stuart and some other photo-interpreters. At first, Stuart judged the information to be an "artifact"—something impressed on the image by an electronic anomaly in the satellite sensing system. The photo-interpreters quickly and efficiently refuted this by dragging out a detailed map and other satellite images of the Hatteras area. Where the "circle" appeared on the photo, the map showed Mattamuskeet Lake. This body of water is bordered on one side by an isthmus of land between the lake and Pamlico Sound, on the other side by a slightly raised isthmus of land between the lake and the swamp.

The conclusion of the interpreters? The relatively low resolution of ESSA 8 made the lake with its surrounding isthmuses appear nearly circular.

When I recalled to Mr. Stuart that the "mystery circle" mentioned in the magazine article was *white*, not dark, the scientist did oblige me by producing an ESSA 8 photo of the Hatteras area revealing very distinctly a white circle. Still refusing to be caught in anything too "Triangle-phenomenon-labeled," Locke Stuart assured me, "Clouds! Weather conditions in that area leave no doubt in my mind that this circle is a cloud formation, not uncommon to Pamlico Sound."

Not nearly so convinced that all satellite photos from the Triangle area can be so patly interpreted—in his particular experience, anyway—is a physics instructor at Longwood College in Farmville, Virginia, named Wayne Meshejian.

The studious physics professor Meshejian boldly proclaimed to the world in the spring of '75 that, as a result of the behavior of the polar-orbiting weather satellites belonging to the National Oceanic and Atmospheric Administration (NOAA) which he has been plotting for three years, he is personally convinced that there is some mysterious electromagnetic force in the Bermuda Triangle. It is a force so powerful it is blocking out signals from weather satellites 800 miles up!

Meshejian explains that the satellites are constructed to transmit infrared pictures which show hot and cold fronts and clear visible pictures which show the earth and its cloud formations as seen by man's eye. The infrared picture is sent directly to earth, while the visible picture is stored on magnetic tape to be transmitted a fraction of a second later.

In the case of the three satellites which have been launched since 1972, the visible pictures in every one of them, began to black out over the Triangle within five months of reaching orbit.

"In the beginning," says Meshejian, "there is nothing wrong. Then we notice a disturbance start to occur. It lasts for half a minute, then a minute, then it blacks out entirely. This has occurred in the same way with each of the three satellites . . . and they occur only when the satellites are over the Triangle.

"Now, it's normal to expect electronic devices eventually to grow weak and stop. But it isn't normal for each satellite to begin weakening only when it goes over the Bermuda Triangle. I say there is some electromagnetic force out there—and it must be an enormous one to erase a tape that is in a satellite 800 miles up!"

Officials with the National Environmental Satellite Service guarantee "there's nothing in the Bermuda Triangle, any more than there's a hole in the North Pole as some people think."

But Meshejian feels he has hit on something that cannot be brushed aside that easily. "NOAA satellites have been misbehaving for the last three years. It's not just my receiver, either. Anyone in range will notice."

Jack Glover, an assistant technical director with the National Environmental Satellite Service, suggests the signals may be weakened by interference from the Wallops Island Station, caused by reading out data while the satellite is overhead. Or another satellite is interfering with the signal.

But Professor Meshejian contends there is "no way the visible photograph is interfered with by other impulses." As controversy grows, Meshejian's untiring efforts to prove his point increase.

"I called an official with NOAA," relates the college professor. "He told me the government was responsible for the blackouts.

"Well, that is highly incredible. The whole purpose of our weather satellites is being defeated if they black out over the United States—where we are the most interested in the weather. I have seen our satellites black out when they go over the Triangle, and when they come back around the world, they're still blacked out. They've stayed blacked out over heavily populated areas such as Denver and Chicago. Would that make sense for the government to "dump" its taped information over areas where it's most needed? No, for the government to do such a ridiculous thing would be contrary to the program's design and purpose. I don't believe such an explanation. If those are the best shots the government can come forth with to put my findings down, then they're hurting!

"To me," concludes Wayne Meshejian, "these satellite blackouts prove that there's a vast electromagnetic force out there in the Triangle and it's of tremendous strength! I'll continue to believe that until the government comes up with real information to prove otherwise."

And, oh yes, if you're wondering, Professor Meshejian just informed me, as of this writing, that NOAA No. 4 is starting to misbehave just as did its predecessors—its signals are beginning to weaken and break up over the Triangle zone!

# Chapter 7

## THE MYSTERIOUS "VOICE"

Francis Wagner has been corresponding with me for some time now. Right from the beginning he described himself and his life as maybe "not making sense" but making one thing clear, he was always "being watched over . . ." or maybe things happened as they did because "he was needed to help others."

One thing *is* clear: Francis Wagner's experiences in World War II and in the years following in the Air Force earned him the reputation of being "the luckiest guy in the Army!"

Wagner was a radio operator. He knew his job expertly. Proof of that was his steady stream of orders to fly VIPs all over the Americas . . . Generals, Attorney Generals, State Department officials, Ambassadors, etc., throughout 1947 and '48.

One such flight exemplified his luck that was to

grow and sharpen with time. He was on a night flight to Jamaica (straight into the Bermuda Triangle, which was unknown to him at the time!) with an experienced pilot, a lieutenant colonel, at the controls. Suddenly the plane's instruments began to malfunction. It was impossible for the pilot or Wagner to ascertain where they were. Clouds began to envelop them, and in desperation, the pilot ordered Wagner to send an SOS.

The radioman shook his head. "No need. Just drop her down. We can land! That's Montego Bay below and we can hit an airfield there!"

The colonel stared, then quietly dropped altitude until they emerged from the cloud bank and could see land beneath. He leveled off and bumped down onto a roughhewn, coral-based airstrip that was in the process of being built.

"How in God's name did you know this was here?" asked the pilot in amazement. "There's never been any notification that this was being constructed—"

"I can't say," said Wagner. "I just suddenly knew, that's all."

Not long afterwards, this same officer and Wagner, plus a full crew, took off for Jamaica again in a B-25. Adventure hit right at the craft when soon after takeoff one of the engines ceased functioning. The men quickly threw out everything they could lay their hands on to lighten the load, but still the plane could not maintain its altitude.

Unable to transfer fuel to the good engine, the colonel ordered Wagner to send an SOS and notify the base they would have to ditch.

Francis Wagner firmly shook his head.

"Don't. We can make it."

"No way, Wagner, we can't. The demand from the one engine for fuel is too heavy . . . we'll be 30 minutes short of making it!"

The radioman persisted, "We'll make it."

"What makes you so sure?"

"It's hard to explain. Something just tells me."

"Okay," said the officer with a wry smile; then, turning to the other men, he asked, "Whad'ya say? Wagner was right about Jamaica before—"

The crew agreed to follow Wagner's hunch.

The B-25 made the field at Jamaica, coughing in for the landing—the last ounce of fuel gone!

The airman shook Wagner's hand as they crossed the field.

"Always listen to that Voice, Wagner, 'cause I'm always going to be listening to you!"

And he did, Francis Wagner recalls to this day. "That colonel seldom took a flight after that unless I was his radio operator."

On another occasion the Voice saved a planeload of men in an experience Wagner has never forgotten.

They were out in a B-25 headed for South America from the U.S. base in Panama when suddenly Wagner blurted out to the pilot that there was something wrong with the right engine.

The lieutenant looked at the radioman as though he were crazy.

"What's wrong? There's no problem with that engine!"

Francis stared at the gauges. They were normal. Still he kept hearing this unspoken insistent warning.

"Better return to base, Lieutenant. I tell you there's something wrong with that right engine!"

The pilot ignored the suggestion.

"You worry too much, Wagner. Kick off. Forget it!"

But Francis Wagner grew more uneasy every second.

Every muscle in his body began to tense with uneasiness when suddenly, to his profound relief, he received a message on his radio.

He nearly yelled the news to the officer. "Return to base, sir! We've just received orders to return to base!"

The lieutenant squirmed in his seat. "What for? There's no reason to go back—confirm that message, Wagner."

The radioman did so. Same thing. "Return to base."

"No mistaking it, sir. We've got to go back."

The craft circled back and hours later roared down on the Panama runway. Just as it hit the field, the right engine "ran away"—it spun the ship out of control and the craft plunged eerily awry. The heart of every man on board was in his throat.

"My God! That *was* a bad engine!" exclaimed the pilot.

Francis Wagner sighed, relieved. Every crew member knew with mounting horror that with a few minutes' difference—if the engine had revved-up in the air—every one of them would now be dead!

But that was not the end of the strange story. When the officer checked into the why's and wherefore's of the order to return to base, he found the weirdest thread of all in the pattern. There had been a mistake made by the ground operator—he had sent the wrong message to them! There had been no order intended for their plane to return to base.

57

Had Francis Wagner's persistent "inner message" affected the base's radio operation?

What happened on board a subsequent flight in that same area Wagner cannot explain, even to this day.

"We were on an experimental trip," recounts the former radioman. "We had an inside gas tank mounted inside the plane. It was a C-47 being tested for long-range flight. Kinda crazy setup, too. An assistant crew chief was flying the plane with the navigator acting as co-pilot. The pilot and co-pilot and the rest of the observers were in the back of the plane playing cards.

"Now, I can't for the life of me tell you why I did what I did—but I suddenly heard this inner Voice and it just took over for me!

"Without saying a word to anyone, I suddenly switched on my radio and began transmitting a series of "T's." This was a signal to alert ground stations that an important message was coming. In such an instance, that frequency is cleared of all messages. All stations copy the messages.

"I then alerted the D/F (direction-finding) stations to get a fix on our plane. I then sent an SOS, giving our position, altitude, pilot's name, plane number, etc.

"Then suddenly, I sat back, shocked at myself. Why had I done such a thing? I had no permission to send an SOS—even worse, no cause! I realized with anguish that I was finished as a radio operator!

"Then at that exact moment, as these thoughts raced through my mind, both engines sputtered and quit!"

The moments that followed are still vivid in Wagner's recollection. The plane nosed into a dive.

The pilot and co-pilot rushed to aid at the controls, and Wagner sent the message that the plane was going down. The pilot, realizing that the plane was out of gas in the special tank, quickly switched to the wing tanks and re-started the engines. Then all four men at the controls pulled with all their might.

Wagner urged the rest of the men to move with him to the back of the plane to equalize the weight somewhat.

"We pulled out just about 60 feet off the ground," recalls Wagner today. "We sheared off a few tree tops, but we made it! And—thank God—we didn't need the emergency setup that had been put into motion by me *minutes before* the emergency occurred!"

Today Francis Wagner shakes his head in wonderment. He can't forget those Air Force days; neither can he explain them. He can only repeat what he has been saying for years: "I was just always being watched over."

Perhaps some Force in the Triangle area, even in the farthest reaches of the Caribbean, affected the instruments or the engines of those Air Force planes, but it's comforting to know that even there, *Something* or *Someone* was there to help.

# Chapter 8

## THE TRIANGLE "CLOUD"

One of the stranger and more inexplicable phenomena of the Bermuda Triangle is what witnesses have variously called a "cloud," a "fog," or a "yellowish haze." This almost mystical materialization is not related to the normal clouds and hazes of our atmosphere. Apparently, this phenomenon appears suddenly and seems to envelop the person or craft, sometimes obliterating it. Witnesses say they have seen a craft disappear in a sudden fog, never to reappear after the mist had dissipated.

In his hardcover book called *The Bermuda Triangle* (not to be confused with my own paperback!) Charles Berlitz recounts the incident of a Captain Don Henry who, in 1966, was towing a barge behind his tugboat from Puerto Rico to Fort Lauderdale when he experienced the weirdest event of his life. All his electric instruments ceased to produce power and, at the same time, he observed that his tow was covered by a cloud while the waves around it became choppier than anywhere else in the environs.

The following few minutes were terrifying. Henry rammed the throttles full ahead, but all he could feel was the effect of some force or some Thing pulling them backwards. He took a quick look back at the towline. It was taut as pulled wire but nothing stretched behind it was in view! Everything was covered by a "fog concentrated around it."

They finally pulled out of the fog, but what astonished Captain Henry was the fact that there was no mist anywhere else! In fact, Henry states that he could see with crystal clarity for 11 miles around!

In June, 1975, newspapers all over our country were carrying the story of two missionaries, Warren and Betty Miller, who flew out of Guatemala headed for Key West, Florida. They, too, ran into that weird fog in the Triangle. To them it appeared as a "yellowish haze."

"We still can't explain what happened," Mrs. Miller told reporters after their safe return to the States. "After leaving the coast of Honduras, we have always, in past trips, very shortly sighted Cuba.

"This time, we couldn't see the island. All we caught sight of was a yellow haze. At the same time, all the plane's dials stopped functioning. My husband made a 30-degree turn which we thought should have put us over Cuba, but still there was only the yellow haze. We'd never seen anything like it."

For almost two hours the Millers floundered in the Triangle looking for land. Flying at 11,000 feet with a dead instrument panel and no radio contact, was, to say the least, unnerving.

Finally, they emerged from the mist; the instruments started working again, and they were able to pick up a signal from Florida which guided them to Key West.

The Millers immediately had their twin-engined Beechcraft E-95 checked out completely. Mechanics said there was nothing whatever wrong with the instrument panel. At Cape Canaveral's airport, they were told the same thing.

"I just can't explain it," says Mrs. Miller, who is also a licensed pilot. "It was very eerie."

Three other travelers in the Triangle did not fare as well as the Millers. Their tragic flight took place on December 16, 1974. Don Parris and Kelly Hanson, two business associates and friends, planned a trip to Haiti to look at some land they were considering buying for development. They engaged an old friend and pilot, Mike Roxby, to fly them down there shortly before the Christmas season got under way.

Mike, an experienced pilot, leased a new blue-and-white single-engine Cessna 172 for the flight. He checked the plane out and found everything in A-1 condition. The controls were fine; the instruments worked perfectly; the weather was superb. The three took off from the airfield of Merritt Island, Florida, at 10:30 a.m. They headed out on a course over the Bahamas.

Before long the craft was over Bimini. Shortly after passing over that island, the plane's instruments started to go haywire. The plane's radios—all four of them—began to black out.

Mike kept his cool, though, and said he'd take directions from the sun. He instructed the other two men to aid him in looking for large islands on the left side—landmarks.

But there was nothing to see but blue water stretching as far as the eye could see.

"It was as though those landmarks had been wiped off the earth," reported Hanson later.

Around 4:30 in the afternoon, the three men sighted a good-sized island. "We decided it was Great Inagua Island," said Parris afterwards. "We were all relieved."

Mike spotted a dirt strip between two sugar cane fields. He dropped down and landed the Cessna with ease. He then checked the fuel with a stick since the gauge was still not functioning. He estimated they had about an hour's flying time left.

While the men were talking, an old farmer was working his way toward them. Two little black-haired children followed in his wake. They were all jabbering in a foreign tongue. Mike turned and talked to them a moment in struggling Spanish. When he looked back at his two friends, his face was white as river foam.

"We're in Cuba!" he blurted out.

The men crawled hastily back into the craft and zoomed upwards as fast as possible.

In the next few minutes, much to Mike's relief, the instruments started working again. The pilot got through to an airliner and was put on a course for Great Inagua.

A moment later, the radios went dead again.

But Great Inagua was unmistakably below them now. Its lighted airstrip was distinct and beautifully welcome. It was just a matter of a few minutes and they'd all be safe on the ground.

Then it happened. Later, neither Parris nor Hanson could explain exactly what occurred in those few frightening seconds. Everything around them was clear as could be, and, suddenly, they were immersed in a swirling cloud that appeared out of nowhere!

Mike last words were, "What the . . .?"

In a split second they were out of the cloud flying in bright clear air, racing directly toward a hillside! The next thing Parris and Hanson knew, they were crawling out of the plane's wreckage. Mike Roxby was dead.

Pilot friends of Roxby's were interviewed after the tragedy. Not one of them could understand what could have happened.

"Roxby was an experienced flyer," said Don Wilson, manager of the Merritt Island airport. "There seems to be no obvious explanation for the crash."

Ed Graves, a senior flight instructor at Merritt airport agreed. "Roxby was a darn good flier. Whatever happened out there in the Triangle couldn't have been caused by man or machine."

Parris and Hanson, though suffering a multitude of broken bones, jaws, fractured skull and crushed ribs, survived the ordeal. They lived to tell of their experiences in this mysterious zone where most men's stories have died with them.

It is interesting that this "cloud" phenomenon affected military planes back in 1946. Bob Wagner, formerly of the U.S. Air Force, can tell you about it. His flight record for December 19th of that year details the weird incident that occurred during a flight headed for South America. Five P-47 fighter planes, escorted by a B-25 medium bomber, took off from the U.S. military base at Panama.

Thirty minutes later, the B-25 was back. The pilot told a strange story. As the squadron was flying serenely along, the group of five P-47s suddenly headed into a cloud. When the B-25 saw them emerge, there were only four! One plane was gone! There had been no emergency call received by any of the planes from the P-47 in question. Though they could not sight each other for several minutes, no communications relating to any problems were exchanged.

The Panama base immediately launched a massive search by ships and planes. Hours later, the search planes—B-17 heavy bombers—were ordered back to base. What was discovered? Two of them were missing!

Each B-17 carried twelve men, so now 24 men plus the original fighter pilot were missing. Panama sent the remaining search planes back up to look for the two B-17s that had disappeared.

One sighting of smoke was reported. But nothing was revealed upon investigation. It didn't seem reasonable to assume the smoke could have had anything to do with the missing fighter plane because of the two to three hours' time lapse. Neither did it seem possible that it could be the result of a mid-air collision of the two missing B-17s. The two craft were assigned 200 miles apart, and neither one was in the search area where the smoke had been reported.

Even if the two planes had somehow veered away from their assigned areas, how could they have collided? On a clear day, could two planes filled with 24 men looking out of the windows crash into each other?

Not a trace of the missing three planes or their 25

crew members was ever found. The mystery was particularly puzzling in those days when all the crews were experienced men with World War II combat records—almost all of them high-ranking officers.

Bob Wagner, who was on one of the search planes, said that no smoke had been sighted by his plane. Whoever reported it had to be someone on one of the three planes involved. Not one of the search craft spotted anything similar to smoke. Out of scores of surface craft, PT boats, three Flying Boats, nothing was found. Not even a single piece of wreckage or a life jacket.

Was the "smoke" connected with the B-17s in any way related to the "cloud" in which the first fighter plane disappeared?

What did happen to three military planes and their 25 crew members that day off South America? We will probably never know any more about that mystery than we do about the Lost Flight 19, the squadron of Avenger bombers that vanished off Florida almost exactly a year before.

# Chapter 9

## THE CASE OF THE
## VANISHED TOUR BOAT

In the past decades with the burgeoning popularity of Williamsburg, the town of Hampton, Virginia, not far south of the restored Colonial village, began to find itself a tourist mecca. Accordingly, the town fathers decided to go into the tour business with real zest and accommodation. One of the first steps they took was to establish a tour boat business. The first vessel carried some 38 passengers and was a raving success. But to the delight of the City of Hampton, the little boat was soon woefully inadequate. Every trip, the sightseeing craft was pulling out from the dock leaving half the people behind.

It was clear to Hampton that by then, 1968, they were ready for a good-sized tour boat. The town fathers turned to the Great Lakes region. Large power boats had operated successfully for years and years all over the lakes of Erie, Ontario, and so forth. A lead was soon obtained on an experienced vessel called the *Carol Diane*. Hampton took a good look into her record.

The *Carol Diane* had operated out of Cleveland, Ohio. She had a fine history. She had weathered Great Lakes storms without a shudder of an anchor link. She was stout of frame and handsome to look upon. She could accommodate 100 passengers. She had at one time plied the waters off Florida without a single mishap. She looked like just what Hampton was searching for. After an in-depth investigation that occupied the town fathers more completely than did the preliminaries for the Hampton coliseum, the decision was made to buy the Great Lakes vessel.

Next, the city made detailed provision to establish conclusively that the Erie boat was safe in every aspect. The local Coast Guard was asked to contact the Cleveland area Coast Guard regarding the worthiness of the vessel for service in the Chesapeake Bay area. This duty, it was agreed, posed no problem for the hardy tour boat.

One investigator recommended more watertight bulkheads. His suggestion was immediately carried out. Marine surveyors called for a new two-way radio. It was installed. The Great Lakes Diesel Corporation checked the engines. They were pronounced in excellent condition. One of the most renowned marine surveyors in the world, at the request of Hampton, made a special trip to Cleveland to double-check the findings. He returned with a ten-page report detailing his investigation, pronouncing the *Carol Diane* completely checked out and one hundred percent seaworthy.

Next, the City of Hampton examined the most experienced men they could possibly choose for the job of running the *Carol Diane*. They hired two of the top seamen in the Chesapeake Bay area.

Luther Perry was well-known along the Virginia coastline. He'd worked the Hampton-Chesapeake waters for many years, having served ably as captain of the original *Kickatan* clipper. He accepted the commission to command the *Carol Diane*.

Mike Byer was one of the finest navigators in the area. He had a second mate's ticket and was happily hired for mate on the new tour boat.

By May of 1968 all was in readiness for the initial voyage of the freshly overhauled vessel. The various departmental bureaus of Hampton had each contributed its time and ideas for the maiden voyage. The fanfare and preparation included appointing Pat Paulsen honorary captain; negotiations for the Smothers Brothers to appear for the launching in addition to the mayor of Hampton, all its town fathers, a uniformed band, and a bevy of expectant newspapermen—all of whom formed a miniscule gathering compared to the ever-swelling knots of tourists awaiting the big moment.

The *Carol Diane's* arrival was pretty closely defined. She had left Cleveland for the 1000-mile journey to her new port under the guiding hands of Perry and Byer. Her route took her to Buffalo, then through the Erie barge canal linking into the Hudson River from where she entered the Atlantic Ocean near Atlantic City. Then she traveled down the coastal waters headed for Hampton Roads. The night before her scheduled arrival, she put in till dawn at Newport News. Perry reported in to Hampton from that final stop, declaring he'd arrive the next day right on time. He'd had a little engine trouble, but nothing serious. It had been taken care of with no difficulty. He'd be tooting in to Hampton right on schedule. That was the last word any one ever heard from Luther Perry or Mike Byer.

In the early morning the vessel cut breezily through the Atlantic Ocean. Newport News sailors watched the shining boat curiously as she churned by. They were the last mortals to lay eyes on the *Carol Diane*. She swept out into the blue waters and disappeared from sight—forever.

The crowd on the dock at Hampton awaited with instruments and voices ready to blare a welcome to the city's new tour boat. As the hours ticked by and no vessel loomed into sight, gradually the people dispersed, a wonder and a heaviness in their hearts.

A vast search was put into swing immediately. Craft of all kinds joined in the hunt. Planes crisscrossed the area looking for the lost vessel. Not a trace of her could be spotted, nor sign of her life raft. There had been no problem weather, no Maydays on the emergency frequency. There had been absolutely nothing. The noble and good-sized tour boat had simply vanished!

Many people to this day shake their heads in bewilderment at the loss of the beautiful ship that was to give so much joy. And many are still too sorrowful and too touched by the loss of Perry and Byer to discuss the incident.

What befell the *Carol Diane* is still unknown. Fragments were found floating days afterward—her name plate and one life preserver. But neither bore testimony as to what had happened. She is one more sad statistic in the annals of Bermuda Triangle losses —all mysteries with no clues to explain the tragedy.

# Chapter 10

## INTO THIN AIR

A sailor with the strangest of strange stories to tell once contacted me.

He had, some years prior, served on a luxury liner cruising between New York and Bermuda.

On one voyage of this popular cruise, the sailor noticed a woman who sat all through the day in a reclining chair on the sun deck close to the rail and quite apart from others.

She wore an orange cotton dress and a silk scarf pulled around her black hair. Large dark glasses rested on her nose. She seemed always to be staring out to sea when he passed by.

Several times in the morning he spoke to her. She scarcely looked his way.

On the last day of the voyage, he noticed her in

her accustomed place as he hurried by on a duty. On his return, she was gone.

A few hours later, after the last dinner sitting, the sailor was called to the captain's quarters along with a score of other seamen. It seemed one of the passengers was missing!

Without arousing any alarm among the voyagers, the captain was going to turn the ship around and see if there was a sign of anybody overboard!

The graceful liner circled around and searched through the course it had just run. The gently heaving waters were without a sign or clue of anyone at all. Once again, the liner switched directions and continued on to Bermuda.

The missing passenger was never found. But my sailor friend realized with a strange pang that it was the interesting lady who was gone. She had scarcely left the sun deck until, without ceremony or fanfare, she left it forever. Later, as the liner nudged into Hamilton, the sailor wondered sadly whether or not the lady in the orange dress had *intended* to go over the rail.

A year went by. The unhappy incident on board the ship was long forgotten. Then came the same cruise date for that year, corresponding to the identical one the previous year. The popular vessel cut through the green sea once again, headed for Bermuda.

The afternoon before the ship was to dock at Hamilton, the sailor strode quickly along the sun deck to accomplish a chore when something brought him stock still in his tracks,—there in a reclining deck chair, close to the rail, off by herself, was the same lady in an orange dress and a silk scarf pulled around her dark hair! She wore sunglasses and was staring out to sea!

The sailor nearly stumbled as he leaned toward her.

"Ma'am—could I get you anything?"

The woman never turned. She said not a word. Her head never moved. In fact, her whole body seemed motionless.

After dinner, the sailor walked past once again in the cool of the evening. The chair was empty. When the ship docked, he scanned the passengers to catch a glimpse of her. He never saw her again.

It was an experience he'd wondered about ever since. It was so eerie, he never mentioned it to any of the crew or the captain. In fact, he'd not dared to share the strange story with anyone before.

Did it, he asked me, have anything to do with the Bermuda Triangle phenomenon?

Perhaps. One of the characteristics of this mysterious zone seems to be the disappearance of people from vessels. I had never heard of a case, however, in which one reappeared.

One of the classic cases of mysterious disappearance is the incident of the *Carol A. Deering* which I covered in my *Bermuda Triangle* book. The five-masted schooner was found deserted—apparently abruptly abandoned by the entire crew in 1921 off Cape Hatteras.

Not a few instances of unaccountable abandonment seem to have occurred in the Triangle. In one brief ten-day period in July of 1969 four boats ranging in size from 20 to 60 feet were found at different locations in the Atlantic between the Azores and Bermuda. In each case, although hundreds of miles apart, the boats had been abandoned. In each

74

circumstance, nothing was found awry on board. All was in order. No evidence of violence or struggle. During the time, there had been no bad weather, which added to the mystery. What had caused the crews of all four boats in a short span of time to abandon them completely without any word of distress and without leaving the smallest clue?

Regarding this inexplicable "rash" of abandonment, Lloyd's of London was quoted by one publication in the U.S. as stating, "It's rare to get reports like these in such a close area in such a vast ocean. It is rather odd."

One of the most fascinating tales of unexplained disappearance was recounted to me by an oldtime seaman named Oscar T. Hines. The weird event took place in 1926 when Hines served on board the U.S.S. *Henderson.* The *Henderson,* Hines told me, was named for Archibald Henderson, who was born in Fairfax County, Virginia, in 1783. He served with the United States Marine detachment on the U.S.S. *Constitution* (Old Ironsides) during her famous victories in the War of 1812.

The officer's namesake was made of stuff such as the old Marine colonel himself could not have imagined. She displaced 7750 tons. She was over 483 feet long and had a beam of 61 feet. Her draft was over 16 feet aft, her cruising speed 14 knots. She sported oil-fired boilers, twin screws turned by triple-expansion reciprocating steam engines, and she was armed with quick-firing naval rifles.

The warship had a crew of 2333 officers and men and troop berthing quarters for 1695 plus stables below for 24 horses or mules. In other words, she could carry a full battalion of field artillery troops, horses, and guns.

The *Henderson* was launched at the Philadelphia Navy Yard on June 17, 1916. She participated in active duty all through World War I. Following the Armistice, the stout vessel made eight more voyages bringing back some 10,000 veterans.

From 1919 on, she took up duty as a troop transport for Marines in the Caribbean. She carried men in that branch of the service and their dependents to Guantanamo, Puerto Rico, Haiti, and other islands. She later expanded her service to ferrying troops to far-flung bases, especially those in the Far East.

It was in the spring and summer of 1926. The staunch vessel was taking a load of Marines for replacement duty for the Legation Guard at Peking, China, and Oscar Hines reported for duty aboard her upon her arrival in San Diego.

The captain was a tall, slim man who had an unusually good rapport with his men. He was extremely well liked, Hines learned. That was understandable. He was not an officer to hold aloof from his crew. He seemed personally interested and concerned about each of his men.

To this day, Oscar Hines can recall his captain's geniality.

"During that voyage, he would come into the radio cabin frequently, and say a word or two to me. I was very impressed. It wasn't often that a Four Stripes showed any sign of friendship to an underling such as me—at least, that had been my past experience."

In midsummer of '26 the *Henderson* was ordered to Haiti, where it was to pick up a full company of Marines. From Coco Solo then, the ship set a straight course for Haiti.

Oscar Hines recalls that voyage vividly. No doubt,

he reasons, the ship's navigator conferred with the captain about sailing directions. They would run the channel between Jamaica and Haiti, then finally head for the Windward Passage and thence to Norfolk, Virginia.

Hines pulled the midnight to 4 a.m. watch in the radio cabin which was on the boat deck just aft of the captain's quarters. Shortly after the young sailor went on watch, the captain came into the radio room. He peered into the darkness ahead.

"Ship's rolling pretty heavy, isn't she, son?" He put a hand on Oscar's shoulder as he sat with the earphones on his temples. "Wind's dead astern. Warm as purgatory, though!"

Oscar looked up and smiled. "Yes, Cap'n."

The tall officer turned then and bent through the cabin door. "I'm leaving word on the bridge to be called from my quarters the moment a light is picked up on the coast of Haiti. Should be around 0400—"

With these words, the captain disappeared into the darkness outside. Hines could hear his feet clicking down the deck toward his cabin. It was the last time Oscar Hines or anyone else ever laid eyes on the *Henderson's* captain.

A message was sent to the ship that night, ordering the vessel to proceed to San Juan, rather than Haiti. That message was never received.

"For some reason," Hines told me, "communication with the San Juan naval radio was very difficult. I missed the dispatch and so we continued on to Haiti."

As Hines was going off duty at 4 in the morning, he saw the bridge messenger pass him going to call the captain. A short time later the young radioman heard the startling news that the captain was nowhere to be found. The entire ship was searched thoroughly. The captain had apparently vanished into thin air!

"I can't believe his disappearance had anything to do with any devil in any Triangle," declares Oscar Hines today. "He could have had a heart attack and fallen over the rail. Perhaps the officer discovered an intruder in his cabin who overpowered him and threw him overboard."

"Was any sign of him or his clothing ever found? Ever spotted in the water or washed up on any shore?" I asked.

Hines responded that there was not.

"But whatever happened in that ocean in 1926," he said, "I am sure it was natural—just one of those risks one takes when one goes to sea."

Oscar Hines proceeded on the *Henderson* to San Juan and thence north to Norfolk where he was released from duty, his term of enlistment having expired.

But the curious instance in which the captain of his vessel—the finest officer he'd ever served—vanished from mortal sight in the Caribbean will never quite fade from his memory.

As with the strange lady on the cruise ship and after scores of other unaccountable disappearances in the Triangle Zone that have followed—no one has supplied any sure answers.

# Chapter 11

## "PHANTOM JET"

It was only four days after Christmas, Friday night, the 29th of December, 1972.

It would be known as Black Friday in the annals of air history.

Not one of the 176 persons aboard the giant airliner had a glimmer of impending disaster as the huge craft approached Miami, its final destination. Most of them were returning from festive holiday reunions, and they were filled with sparkling recollections.

The pilot and co-pilot had no time for such casual preoccupations. They were preparing to bring the huge craft down over the Everglades and onto the runway at Miami International Airport.

Flight control ordered an automatic pilot altitude maintenance of 2000 feet. Just as the jet was in sight of Miami, a light flickered on the control panel. Instantly, the pilot ordered cancellation of the landing.

"Gear trouble!" he called out.

But there proved to be nothing wrong with the gear. It was a faulty indication. The pilot announced he wished to make a go-around for a second landing attempt.

Then came the first indication of any alarm related to this Tri-Star Jumbo Jet No. 310.

A traffic controller monitoring the flight as it was preparing for a second approach noticed it was flying at an excessively low 837 feet. He radioed to the plane's crew, "What is your status now?"

"Okay," came the reply. "We'd like to turn around and come back in."

The jet made its turn and re-approached. Seconds later the air split apart with a tremendous roar. The craft was headed straight for the Everglades! One thing was clear, the crewmen were applying full power in that last desperate moment to pull out of their fatal descent.

It was futile. Nothing could halt the downward thrust. Within seconds the swamps were bombarded with thundering metal parts, tearing steel, bits of split fuselage, wings, plane seats—

A stewardess opened her eyes and staggered out of the wreckage. She gazed around her, stunned. Mud and blood covered everything.

Recalling those moments of horror later, she said, "There was only terrible silence with water dripping!"

It was a holocaust. The disaster was pronounced the worst in the history of Miami Airport. By final count, 101 out of 176 died in the fatal crash.

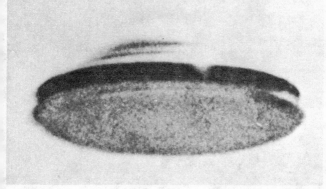

**Top:** Robert de la Parra of New Jersey on a sail off Cape Hatteras just prior to the weirdest experience of his life in the Devil's Triangle. **Above:** Flying Saucers such as this are witnessed frequently over the Devil's Triangle area by residents of the coastal areas —particularly Florida and Bermuda. Also by seamen such as Lloyd Frederick of California while on the U.S.S. Murray in 1954. Frederick described his UFO as looking like *"a gigantic jellyfish."*

**Below:** Andie Gorman of Pennsylvania, who works frequently with such problem-probers as the U.S. Navy at Annapolis, has spotted strange forms and eerie lights in Bermuda Triangle waters. **Right:** David Swanner of Tennessee points to the spot in a forest clearing where a UFO landed and picked him up for a ride a short time before. Stanley Ingram, columnist for the *Pulaski Citizen,* looks on. *Photo courtesy of The Pulaski Citizen, Pulaski, Tenn.*

North ↑

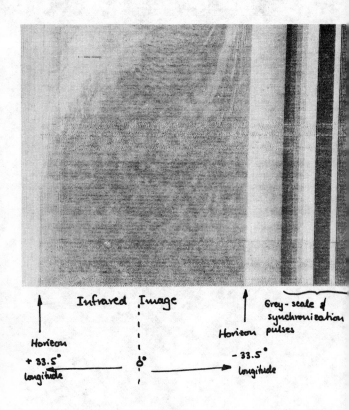

Infrared Image

Grey-scale of
synchronisation
Horizon pulses

↑
Horizon

+ 33.5°
Longitude

0°

− 33.5°
Longitude

A typical blackout of the visible image occuring
over the Triangle area. Note that both
synchronisation pulses and imagery are

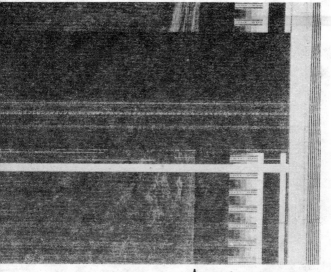

Visible Image     ↑        grey-scale &
                Horizon    synchronization
                           pulses

blacked out. Thus, even when the visible image
is dark (as in this picture), a malfunction is
easy to detect.

**Below:** Jim Martenhoff, Boating Editor of the *Miami Herald*, a confirmed disbeliever in UFO's, changed his mind after a chilling experience in the Devil's Triangle. **Right:** Lloyd and Jean Wingfield in their power boat that took them to sea off Lighthouse Point, Florida and to remarkable adventure ...an encounter with an Unidentifiable Submersible Object *(USO)* in the Devil's Triangle. **Bottom Right:** Satellite photos have been showing possible mysterious results. This photo of ESSA 8 shows a "white circle" *(arrow)*. Is it due to a cloud formation or is it an example of the Triangle's mysterious "*Circles of Light?*"

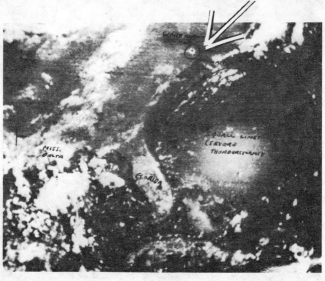

**Top:** A U.S. Airforce C-47 cargo plane of World War II. Radioman Francis Wagner was on an experimental flight of this craft (a gas tank was mounted inside the plane) to test it for long range flight when the *"Voice"* took over in the Triangle Zone and saved the plane and its crew from certain death. **Left:** Radioman Wagner when stationed in Panama in 1947. Because an inner *"Voice"* guided him and protected him from disaster, he was dubbed "the luckiest guy in the army." It saved him from death several times in the Devil's Triangle.

**Top:** In the foreground a B-17 bomber. Two of this type of craft disappeared off Panama in 1947 while searching for a missing fighter plane that had vanished in a cloud. **Right:** A broken hull and a lone life preserver washed ashore at Virginia in May of 1968 . . . stark testaments to the existence of the vanished tour boat. the *Carol Diane. Photo courtesy of the Daily Press. Newport News. Virginia*

**Top:** An L1011 Tri Star jumbo jet. a "sister ship" to the giant craft that crashed into the Florida Everglades on December 29, 1972. thereby creating not only disaster. but a ghostly legend. **Right:** Dick Rath. editor of *Boating* magazine and an experienced sailor who found his command on a freighter some years ago included coping with a haunted engine room.

Cunard's Queen Elizabeth II when "caught" in the Bermuda Triangle area in April of 1974. She was rendered helpless about 187 miles southwest of Bermuda. The passengers were rescued by the Sea Venture. This and the following photos were taken during rescue operations by Kramer Schatzlein, a passenger.

The Sea Venture, rescuing heroine of the QEII.

**Top:** Rescue operations being effected during the stalling of the QEII in the Devil's Triangle. **Above:** Mrs. Kramer Schatzlein on board the *Sea Venture* after being taken off the stranded QEII.

A little over two months later, the board of inquiry presented its report.

A test of the automatic pilot failed to turn up any malfunction, yet that system which would have held the plane at its assigned 2000 feet wasn't engaged when the plane hit the ground. Still, the investigators stated that they were convinced that the co-pilot had activated it earlier as instructed.

What had disengaged the automatic pilot system?

There is no concrete answer. Only a guess that possibly when the pilots were occupied with checking out the cockpit warning light that had given a faulty indication of gear trouble and caused cancellation of the first landing, one of them may have inadvertently disengaged the autopilot's altitude-hold function.

It seems the only plausible solution. Unless one stops to consider that Jet No. 310 was on the border of the Bermuda Triangle where so often, without explanation, instruments cease to function properly.

Other mysteries emerged from the examination of the jumbo jet disaster. The recorders showed that in the last two minutes of flight, as the plane descended, its airspeed increased along with its downward pitch. During those few minutes, there was a series of puzzling throttle reductions which hastened the craft's descent. Had the automatic system brought about the reduction in power? The investigators made no attempt to explain that power cutback.

Another puzzle: the voice recorders gave no hint that any of the crew ever sensed trouble, not even after being questioned about their status by traffic control. Not until the craft had nearly struck ground did they become aware of their altitude and attempt to pull out of the dive.

All of these questions were left without positive answers by probes of the National Transportation Safety Board and the Federal Aviation Agency.

But even stranger aspects of this crash were yet to unfold.

It seems that the big airliner that was scheduled to take the New York–to–Miami run that December night was not No. 310, but No. 318. At the last minute, 310 was substituted for her "sister ship."

And that set the stage for very peculiar problems.

No. 318, it was reported to me, is haunted!

Shortly after the Everglades tragedy, while the Miami crew was ferrying 318 back to Miami from Atlanta, an inexplicable thing happened. One engine went off, then came back on—for no apparent reason.

On a subsequent flight of 318 not long after, another strange thing occurred. Without reason, the lights went off, then came back on—for no apparent reason.

All that was only the beginning.

A few months later at Philadelphia Airport, a mechanic boarded this same craft to check its logbook where flight problems are listed. The report was signed by each of the present crew of 318, but after the last name appeared a signature that sent the mechanic reeling back. It was the signed name of the co-pilot of old 310!

Not long after that incident when the 318 plane was on the New York–to–Miami run, one of its stewardesses descended alone in the tiny elevator to the galley in the lower level of the jumbo craft. As she stepped around the corner from the elevator toward one of the ovens, she froze to a standstill. A figure was standing in front of the circuit-breaker panel to one side!

She had never seen the man before. He was a first officer, as she could tell from the three gold stripes on the sleeve of his black uniform. He was middle-aged, slightly graying, and his eyes were the saddest ones she had ever seen in her life.

As the stewardess opened her mouth to speak to him, to ask him why he was down there and who he was, the figure faded and was gone from sight!

Terrified, the girl rushed into the elevator and back up to the upper level. She refused ever to go down again to the galley alone. In fact, I was told, no stewardess on that craft would ever again go to the galley by herself. They always went in pairs.

Although the stewardess had never met the co-pilot of No. 310, she described him, associates said later, to a "T."

Stewardesses are not the only ones to be ghost-observers on this particular craft. A caterer delivering the meals to the galley once came flying out—the face of a man had peered back at him from the door of oven No. 6!

Several stewardesses agreed with him. They told me of seeing this same face in the door of that particular oven several times.

On one occasion a stewardess scorned all fears and rushed down in a hurry during a meal hour. There was the face in No. 6! This time the ghostly mouth opened.

"Fire! Fire!" it called.

She dropped the tray and ran.

"I think it was that first officer of No. 310. He

99

was trying to warn me of something. Possibly that oven was about to catch fire. I don't know," she said.

Other stewardesses related one further phenomenon that reoccurs in the galley of this plane. From time to time (in an area where the noise is enormous —I can testify to that myself!) there is a sudden dead silence. "The roar of the engines—everything—goes off. There isn't a sound!"

"Just as it was right after the crash that night in the Everglades!" added another girl.

The airline finally decided to take action. I was told by several crew members that the company had sent the plane back to Lockheed with orders to change the door on oven No. 6.

Still the troubles on No. 318 continued. Just prior to one flight a captain saw the apparition of the old co-pilot and refused to take the flight.

One interesting factor; these ghostly incidents occur only to the Miami-based crews. But even that seems to be sufficient doomsday-calling. The last I heard, Tri-Star Jumbo Jet No. 318—the one true "Phantom Jet"—had been mothballed. She lies stored away in some Florida hangar, unseen, unheralded, unsung, and *most* unknown.

# Chapter 12

## WHAT CAME ABOARD?

Dick Rath is a soft-spoken, level-headed man. But he can tell you an inexplicable tale that occurred within the Triangle that he will never forget.

It goes back to some years ago when Dick was given his first commercial ship command. He was to captain an old rinky-dink freighter that had more history within its rattling bones than any volume by Samuel Eliot Morison.

The vessel was, in Rath's words, "an ugly, cranky little freighter" by the name of TMT *Lloyd*. She had earned her living for many previous years carrying container cargo between San Juan and the U.S. Virgin Islands. But neither her cargo nor her crew had fared too well during her lifetime—or to phrase it more accurately, perhaps one should say, her "death-time."

Yes, from the time of her christening, this perverse old freighter created death-havoc with mankind. Reportedly, one man had been killed during her construction. He was number one.

Then there was the incident on a Caribbean wharf when one of the dock workers was killed loading cargo on the testy little freighter.

He was number two.

But it seems to be numbers three, four, and five that formed the heart of the strange world of the TMT *Lloyd*. Their disaster and their trauma did not die with the men themselves . . . so it is said on waterfronts from St. Thomas to Puerto Rico.

The fatal incident goes back to many years ago when the freighter ran into one of those famous Caribbean storms that pound and thrash and beat mercilessly about a ship. The quivering freighter didn't take kindly to battering. She groaned and heaved and rolled until, with one quick sweep like the flick of a whiplash, she tossed completely upside down, totally capsized. Most of the crew escaped with their lives—even the old *Lloyd* itself was righted and sent back into service again eventually.

But not three of her crew. They never saw service again except with Davy Jones. They had been in the engine room at the time of the capsizing and were trapped beneath the vessel down in the depths of the Atlantic, never to breathe the earth's air again.

The bizarre tragedy seemed to have left its mark on the course of the tin-Lizzie *Lloyd*. The old ship was never the same again. For one thing, she would roll like a barrel over Niagara in the slightest frisky sea. For another thing, her two engines became so touchy they would overheat in no time at all. When one gave out first, as was usually the case, the old freighter reacted like a confused rat in a maze. She would refuse to steer in anything but huge circles.

But her biggest hang-up was her "phantom crew!"

Dick Rath almost guffawed in the serious faces of his Puerto Rican crew on the day he first took command of the *Lloyd* and was informed that the ship was haunted.

He restrained his laughter when he looked at the men's weather-etched faces, drawn and solemn, as they stated in dead earnest, "There are ghosts in the engine room. They appear regularly. They are the spirits of the three men who died trapped in the engine room when she capsized years ago. They will not leave the ship. They will stay with it forever!"

Dick pursed his lips, thought a moment, then asked, "Why do they keep hanging around? Don't tell me they *like* it here?"

One of the crew replied quickly with a firm shake of his dark head, "They keep coming back to warn us—warn every crew that comes aboard—"

Rath raised his eyebrows.

"Warn? Of what?"

"Of another capsizing, Captain Rath. This freighter will capsize again. The ghosts know it. They don't want anyone else to suffer their fate."

Another crewman spoke up, "Most Puerto Ricans will not sail on the *Lloyd*. We are afraid, too, Captain, but—" with a shrug—"one must earn a living. . ."

Captain Rath inspected the engine room. It was nothing to brag about in any Navy Club, but it appeared as sound as one could expect in a freighter of her age.

Old Cando, the first mate, didn't bother to complain about the worn freighter's functions, but neither was he exactly secure. He had, the captain learned, a rather disconcerting habit. Regularly, every night, Cando hung bedsheets over his cabin window.

"Hey, mate, doesn't that make it kinda stuffy for sleeping?" Dick asked him one day.

Cando agreed that it did, but he had to do it all the same "for peace." "Can't get to sleep, Capitan, if I don't."

Rath just stared uncomprehending.

The mate glanced toward the galley, his eyes opening wide. "The noise the ghosts make—it's very loud. They're zombies. They keep running in and out of the galley all night and keep waking me up every time they pass by my window!"

Rath pushed his cap back on his head.

"Hmm. Do the zombies frighten you, Cando?"

"No, Capitan, they do not frighten me. I am too used to them. We are old neighbors, the zombies and I. I have grown up with them, sailed schooners with them, shared quarters with them. I know them well. They do not come to hurt me or any man—they come for revenge."

"Revenge?" Rath found himself intrigued.

Cando nodded. "For the men who died in the engine room. For all men who have died in these waters, they come to revenge. They will kill this ship. They want only to break her, doom her, sink her forever. Some day they will."

The rest of the crew exchanged tales about the old freighter's haunted engine room at the slightest opportunity. Most of the stories related to mechanical difficulties in the engine room. The ghosts, they declared, took particular delight in opening the valves in the ballast manifold, causing the water ballast to flow from one tank to another. Whenever this occurred, the men would look knowingly at each other and comment, "The ghosts are trying to sink the ship!"

The *Lloyd* was at sea for several weeks before any further problems arose. Then one night something happened that spelled trouble, with a capital T, for Captain Rath's voyage.

He was asleep, off watch, when he was awakened by a loud commotion on deck. Cando was at the helm, Rath found, and four crew members were hovering around the cargo, flicking flashlights excitedly around the containers. They were gesticulating and calling to each other in frightened tones.

"It's the zombies, Capitan," explained the mate simply. "They woke you up, didn't they?"

Dick Rath turned disgustedly. "What woke me up was a bunch of superstitious sailors running around screaming at each other in the middle of the night!'"

Cando shook his head.

"No, sir. The zombies started the shouting first. The men are only screaming back at them. You see, they are being argumentative because they want the zombies to cease their troublemaking."

"Troublemaking?" Rath scratched his head in disbelief.

"Yes, sir. The zombies tried to loosen the turnbuckles on the containers. That is dangerous."

Rath shook his head in hopelessness. It was useless, he thought, to explain that what was loosening the turnbuckles was the *Lloyd*'s weak deck. Just as useless as it had been before to explain that what was opening valves in the ballast manifold was vibration.

The captain said nothing. He just turned on his heel and made his way back to bed. It was all too stupid and too hopeless.

The steady opening of the valves in the ballast manifold was too much, however, for the engineer of the *Lloyd*. At the end of the voyage, he quit.

Rath was careful in his hiring of a replacement. He had had it up to his dark level eyebrows with ghosts and zombies. He checked out Louie, a sophisticated New York Puerto Rican, with great care.

"Do you believe in ghosts?"

Louie looked surprised.

"No."

"Do you ever see any?"

"No."

"Well, that's a relief," concluded Dick Rath. "I don't, either. So I guess we won't have any trouble with ghosts on this trip!"

They didn't. Things couldn't have been quieter on the old freighter's next run. Nor on the following one. Everything ran as smoothly as Puerto Rican rum. Rath was pleased, and the old troubles of the engine room began to fade from his memory. Louie proved to be an excellent engineer. All was in top form.

Then came the third voyage.

As was his custom, Louie made it a habit to check the engine room about every half-hour. He examined the oil and water, then would spend the rest of the time in the wheelhouse.

One night, just before dawn and after a rough few hours, as the freighter was approaching St. Thomas, Louie and Rath stood chatting outside the wheelhouse while the cook was steering and the rest of the crew were sleeping in the accommodation directly

106

abaft the wheelhouse. There was a lull in the conversation. Louie glanced at his watch and said it was time to check the engines again. He disappeared down the pipe into the engine room. Rath turned and stared into the darkness. A few minutes later he heard fast footsteps behind him. It was Louie. He was white as a sail and shaking like a stowaway.

Rath reached one hand out. "Louie! What in blazes is wrong? What's happened?"

"Santa Maria, Rath, I *saw* them! And they spoke to me! I know you don't believe in ghosts, and I don't, either, but I swear to you, I *saw* them and I *heard* them!"

"Good Lord, Louie, you can't believe that! Someone's playing tricks on you! Why, I'll bet some crew member was down there—"

Louie shook his head vehemently.

"There was no one down there but me!"

"Now, Louie, you *know* there's no such thing as a ghost—" Dick began again, but the engineer brushed his hand off his arm.

"Maybe not for you, there isn't, but I *saw* them and they *spoke* to me!"

"What did they say?"

"They said, 'Louie, you'd better get out of this engine room. The ship's going over. If you don't get out of here, you'll die just the way we did, trapped in here like rats! Quick, Louie, get out! She's going over!"

Dick persisted in his questioning. It was incredible that someone as sharp as Louie could—

"Tell me, Louie, did they speak to you in English or Spanish?"

"They spoke Spanish, just as clear as anything. I didn't get to check the engines, and I'm not going to, either. I'm never going back down there. I'm quitting. As soon as we reach St. Thomas, I'm leaving and never setting foot on this ship again!" Louie strode around defiantly and leaned over the rail. He sputtered over one shoulder, "If you want those engines checked tonight, you'll have to do it yourself!"

Rath stood watching the Puerto Rican's stubborn back for about ten seconds, then he turned on one heel. First, he checked out the entire crew. He knew where three of them were—all awake on deck. But what of the others? He took a quick look. All were sound asleep in their bunks. Next, he headed for the engine room.

He coughed in the closeness for a moment, then got busy checking the oil and the water—and the ballast valves.

Damn! One was open! It should have been closed . . . how in hell? Had to have opened up from vibration. Had to. That's all there was to it. Yet—

Dick Rath had had enough. He summoned up his best Spanish and yelled at the top of his lungs, drowning out the sound of the engines from his own ears.

"All right, zombies or ghosts or dead seamen or whatever you are—come on out and show yourselves! I'm waiting!"

Nothing happened.

Rath let the curses fly in a flow of bad Spanish, the best he could spurt out in his frustration.

Still nothing happened.

Rath looked around him, then shuddered.

God, he was getting flaky. What kind of nut was he to stand there shouting at no one at all? He went back on deck.

Louie was standing there waiting for him.

"Were they there?"

"No."

"Yes, they were," he insisted.

The next morning, directly after they'd cleared customs in St. Thomas, Louie jumped ship. Flew back to San Juan, Dick heard, and from there made his way back to the States. Dick Rath never saw him again.

Old Cando chuckled when he heard the news.

"Guess the zombies really scared him," he observed philosophically. "That's not hard to understand. But they didn't mean to frighten him, if he'd only understood that. They were only trying to warn him."

The captain glanced at him and said not a word. The whole business had gotten to be too much. He hadn't the energy to respond any more. The zombies were winning out.

Cando spat over the rail. "Yes, sir. It's not hard to understand. It's just a matter of another warning. The old ship is going to capsize again. They'll keep doing that to her until they finally kill her off!"

Rath shook his head in disgust and walked off down the deck.

He could hear Cando's voice still muttering, "They'll get their revenge! You'll see! They'll win!"

Two months later, the company transferred Dick Rath to another ship. He left the *Lloyd* without a backward look. If he had, it would have been his last chance to see the ill-fortuned vessel. Within a week, the doomed freighter capsized and sank while she was at dock in San Juan.

Still determined, the company had her raised and repaired; then they sent her back to sea. That lasted about one year. Then one night she capsized off the coast of Puerto Rico and sank. This time for good.

Whatever haunted that engine room, whatever was on board—every sailor in the Caribbean knew it had won the final battle in a war against one of the most ill-fated vessels that had ever plied those waters—right in the middle of the Devil's Triangle.

# Chapter 13

## DID THE "DEVIL'S SEA" CLAIM AMELIA EARHART?

"Lady Lindy," they called her, the most daring woman of her day. She followed close in the footsteps of Charles Lindbergh, flying the wide reaches of the world's oceans. Her appeal and fame were close to the lanky Lindy's, for, like him, she seemed to go quietly about her business of adventuring into the unknown with as little fanfare as possible. The world loves heroes and heroines like that.

And in that same fashion she launched her final challenge to the skies in 1937. Some of her closest family members were unaware of her plans when Amelia checked in for her final night in Boston at the Copley Plaza. From there she wrote her sister and told her of the flight she would be making the next day. It was the last letter she ever wrote.

The flight was the aviatrix's most ambitious. She

had flown the Atlantic solo five years before in 1932, winning worldwide acclaim as the first woman to accomplish such a feat. In 1935 she flew across the Pacific. But all this was not enough. She wanted to circle the globe in one sweeping equatorial flight. She set early summer of 1937 as the date.

For her companion on this near 30,000-mile trip, she chose an enthusiastic navigator named Fred Noonan, who eagerly accepted the challenging assignment even though he had married only a few months before the scheduled departure date.

Her craft was equally reassuring to Amelia Earhart. It was a stout twin-engined silver monoplane equipped with a radio transmitter capable of sending messages over a 1000-mile distance. It was so constructed that should she run out of gas over the ocean, the empty fuel tanks would keep it floating for hours. It was the *Electra*.

Amelia Earhart checked out of the Copley Plaza that morning in May and took off for Oakland, California, her starting point for the equatorial flight around the globe. She and Noonan breezed up into the skies over southern California on May 20, 1937, right on schedule.

They flew first to Miami, then pushed on toward the east as the world listened and waited for progress reports at each leg of the journey. By early July, the *Electra* was dropping down onto an airfield on the Pacific island of New Guinea. The two fliers were tired, plane-weary, and bleary-eyed. But they were also exhilarated by their achievement: they'd flown 22,000 miles. Only the last leg of the planned flight remained, a mere 7000-mile lap. But the last was not the least in importance. Both Amelia and Fred knew it was the biggest challenge. Ahead of them lay a huge expanse of ocean with their refueling point a tiny speck of an island called Howland. Finding it would require the most accurate navigational reckoning.

The two fliers had pored over Howland's geographical characteristics and its pinpoint position in the Pacific Ocean. The tiny strip was only twenty miles long and three quarters of a mile wide. Its greatest height above sea level was only fifteen feet. Amelia and Fred knew their reckoning had to be exact. Each mile they might take off course would add up to forty miles on the distance to be covered to Howland!

On the stroke of the scheduled second of July 2nd, the silver plane lifted off the airfield at Lae, New Guinea. It was precisely 10 a.m. The *Electra* winged out gracefully toward the wide waters of the South Pacific. Amelia and Fred felt a surge of joy in getting off on the last lap. A weary and anxious mother and sister awaited Amelia in Boston and a devoted husband also, the well-known publisher, George Palmer Putnam. And Fred was eager to get back to his bride of only three months, Mary.

Almost immediately, though, trouble broke out in the flight. Noonan reported radio difficulties because he was unable to set his chronometers. Neither he nor Amelia wanted to give up the last leg and cut the flight short so near to completion. There wasn't anything serious to worry about, they both agreed, as they would soon be over the islands and atolls of the Gilbert Islands group—highly identifiable landmarks.

It was a little after ten o'clock in the morning. They had cast the die. They were airborne for the 2556 miles to Howland, the last stepping-stone to

Hawaii and the United States—a flight of twenty hours.

The world held its breath waiting for news of the gallant young woman and her companion. The morning of the 3rd of July found a suspense-gripped public anxious for word.

The officers and crew of the U.S. Coast Guard cutter *Itasca* were equally concerned by early dawn of the following day. The cutter was anchored off Howland, waiting to help the aviatrix find the island. But it was now nearly 24 hours since the *Electra* had taken off from Lae and no one had received any word from the craft.

At 7:42 a.m., the radio operator on the cutter drew to rigid attention. A message was coming through from the *Electra!* Amelia Earhart was calling over and over, her voice high-pitched and obviously in despair.

"We must be on you but cannot see you. Gas is running low. We are flying at an altitude of 1000 feet."

"*Itasca* calling," the operator said into his microphone over and over with no acknowledgment from the *Electra*. He recorded the situation in his logbook. But nothing further did he hear for a quarter of an hour; then, once again, he picked up a call from Amelia, her voice even more alarmed in tone, "We are circling you! We cannot hear you! Go ahead on 7500, either now or on scheduled time of half-hour!"

The *Itasca* radio operator immediately tapped out the Morse direction-finding signal on 7500 kilocycles.

There was a quick reply from the *Electra,* "Now we are receiving your signals but are unable to get a bearing. Please take a bearing on us and answer by voice on 3105!"

The radio operator of the cutter began to transmit steadily.

"*Itasca* calling! *Itasca* calling!"

It was a quarter to nine before he received any further word. It was Amelia's voice again cutting in:

"We are in line of position 157-337. We are running north and south. We are listening on 3210 kilocycles!"

The cutter operator changed his frequency and repeated his message. Every man in the radio room strained to listen for further word from the aviatrix or her navigator. None was forthcoming. That brief message from her recorded in the cutter log held the final words ever heard from Amelia Earhart. And it was a message with no meaning. What did 157-337 refer to?

When the radio room of the *Itasca* reported its failure to pick up any further contact from the *Electra*, Captain Thompson of the Coast Guard cutter radioed Washington, "Amelia Earhart missing."

It was the sad word the whole world hoped it would never hear. Its most famous woman aviator had vanished. The greatest air-sea search ever launched for a single plane was put into operation. Seven Navy ships and an aircraft carrier with its planes combed an area of 151,556 square miles for weeks afterward. Not a clue or vestige of anything was found. No bodies, no clothing, no floating debris, no crash remains on any stretch of island anywhere! The *Electra* had disappeared!

Finally and reluctantly, on the 19th of July, the search was called off.

The mystery and the unanswered questions concerning one of the world's greatest mysteries remained. In the 38 years that have lapsed since that fateful flight, investigation has never completely ceased. From time to time, some new piece of possible evidence surfaces, and the lava of curiosity bubbles up again.

In the early wake of the tragedy, theories bounded all over like corn kernels in a bonfire. Amelia and Fred had run off to an abandoned island to be together in a well-hidden romance! There was even an answer supplied by a psychic, a friend of Amelia's who reported "seeing" the *Electra* crash into the sea near a Japanese fishing vessel!

Then there was the "spy theory." Amelia, working for the U.S. Government, was ordered to get lost in the area of Japan's islands, so that vessels from America ostensibly "searching" could be photographing Japanese military bases with ease.

Or the "Secret Service theory." Amelia and Fred were "undercover agents" involved in getting information on America's future enemy, the Japanese. Perhaps the pilot and her navigator were shot down and held as prisoners.

It is interesting that some evidence linking Amelia to the Japanese was brought to light in 1944 when a photo album was picked up by two Marine officers on the Japanese-held Marianas Islands, north of Howland. The album reportedly contained several snapshots of Amelia in flying gear. There was further corroboration when, it is alleged, after the war, U.S. investigators unearthed detailed records of the aviatrix's career stored in the Japanese Navy archives in Tokyo! Why were the Japanese so interested in Amelia Earhart?

Those questions remain unanswered.

But there may be further clues to mull over. One of the most exciting came to light in 1960 when Paul Briand, Jr., wrote a biography of Amelia entitled *Daughter of the Sky*. In it he revealed an interesting story.

In 1946 a naval dentist named Dr. Casmir Sheft, who was in practice on the island of Saipan in the Marianas, was talking in his office with a friend. The two happened to get onto a discussion of the Amelia Earhart mystery. While they were engaged in conversation, a dental assistant of Dr. Sheft's, a Japanese woman named Josephine Blanco, walked by and overheard their comments. She turned on her heel and walked toward them.

"I saw a woman aviator—a white woman—when I was a child—about nine years ago, right here in Saipan."

The two men were open-mouthed with fascination. "When? What happened?" they asked eagerly. "Tell us everything you know!"

"Well," the young woman went on, "this was in about 1937. I was just eleven years old at the time, but I have always remembered the incident."

The two men riveted their attention on the young woman as she continued:

"I was bicycling one day to Tanapag Harbor where my brother-in-law, J. Y. Matsumoto, worked. I was taking him his lunch. I was hurrying because it was nearly noon and I knew he would be hungry and waiting for me.

"As I was pedalling along, I heard the sound of an airplane above me. I looked up, and there was a two-engined silver plane flying low overhead. Suddenly, it swooped and thumped down on its belly in the harbor.

"After I had delivered the lunch to my brother-in-law and was bicycling back through the area that was Saipan's military base (I had a special pass to allow me to pass through that part of the harbor), I saw some Japanese soldiers leading two people off the base toward the woods nearby."

Josephine paused and swallowed. It was clear she was still touched by the memory, thought the two men. She went on:

"I could see the two people very clearly. One was a slim young man; the other was a frail, slender woman. She had on khaki clothes; her hair was cut short like a man's, and her thin features looked very white and drawn. In fact, she looked ill.

"I didn't dare stop pedalling, but I watched as long as I could over one shoulder. The soldiers led the woman and man out of sight into the woods. Just a moment later, I heard two shots ring out; then silence. Afterwards, the soldiers came out alone.

"I was just a child, but I remember it all very well."

A few days later, Dr. Sheft arranged to have Josephine shown photographs of Amelia Earhart and Fred Noonan. She nodded quickly. That was the pair. It was they she had seen that summer day in 1937.

Josephine Blanco's story has been sifted through fine-meshed netting. It has the ring of truth and sincerity. Nor can anyone determine why she should make up such a story. If she were so inventive and eager to be the one to solve the Earhart riddle, why would she have waited almost ten years to give it to the world? It seems clear that what she had seen had no significance to her until she heard her employer discussing a lost American aviatrix.

But nothing was ever found to support Josephine Blanco's testimony. No remains of bodies or clothing remnants. No unheralded graves were brought to light—until 15 years later—when the whole affair surfaced again.

In the fall of 1961 Fred Goerner, an American newsman with radio station KCBS in San Francisco, reported that he had just received word of the existence of a shallow grave on Saipan. The news had come to him from a businessman named Thomas E. Devine of West Haven, Connecticut. Devine had been a G.I. with a post office unit stationed on Saipan from 1944 to 1945. He frequently went for long walks around the island. One day, he was approached by a native woman who asked if he were looking for a grave.

He replied that he was not particularly looking for anything but he'd be interested to take a look. The woman guided him over to a shallow grave filled with the remnants of human bones projecting through the earth. Devine didn't think too much about the significance of such a grave and after kicking a bit around the site, he walked on back to base and never gave it another thought. Years later, when he heard Fred Goerner discuss the old Earhart mystery and a possible expedition to search for her grave, he recalled the incident.

Goerner led an expedition and did, indeed, on September 21st, come upon the burial site on Saipan just where Devine had described it to be. The bones were rushed to Dr. Theodore McCown, professor of Anthropology at the University of California at Berkeley. Were they the long-lost relics of Amelia Earhart and Fred Noonan? Once more, the world awaited an answer to the old mystery. And once more, it was to be disappointed. The bones turned out to be those of an Oriental.

Amelia and Fred were still among the lost.

Today, the disappearance of the two fliers is still a mystery. How might the Devil's Triangle be linked to the puzzle?

Well, the only hard evidence that exists at all points to the fact that the pair were in what is now called the Devil's Sea Triangle—similar to the Bermuda Triangle—an area lying south of Japan and extending farther south to the Marianas Islands (a region so filled with the history of vanished craft that it has been dubbed by the Japanese the "Devil's Sea" and labeled a "Danger Zone").

The "Earhart evidence" is an old plane generator found in Saipan harbor in 1960. It has been identified as possibly being the generator of the lost Electra.

The Earhart plane had just such a generator. From its degree of wear and decomposition, it is estimated as having been in the depths of Saipan harbor for about the length of some 35 years.

But, one may ask, what were Amelia and Fred doing over Saipan harbor?

They could have been there. Putting the pieces of the puzzle together, such a possibility is strong.

The distance from Lae, New Guinea, is almost exactly the same as the distance to Howland. If the two fliers made a mistake in their navigational calculations, they could have flown *north* instead of *east,* almost at right angles to their intended course. That would have been an enormous mistake in calculation, but it had happened before—more than once, in fact. They had several times made a navigational error that was a hundred percent off course.

Had they erred again on the morning of July 2nd, 1937, as they winged upwards from Lae?

A positive answer would solve a few minor mysteries in the case. When Amelia had radioed the Coast Guard cutter that she was 2600 miles from the *Itasca* and thought she had identified the Gilbert Islands below her, she and Noonan could have been flying over the Caroline group instead, just south of the Marianas Islands. These, too, were atolls and coral reefs and would have appeared the same from 1000 feet up.

Now we would also have a solution to a puzzle that no one has ever been able to solve over the years. What was Amelia referring to when she radioed the *Itasca,* "We are in a line of position 157-337?"

It was a cryptic message that meant nothing to the cutter's radio room. All they knew was that she had given it as a clue to her position. It was not a radio bearing. Was it a sun bearing? If it had been, it was of no help to the radio operators, as they did not know her geographic point of reference.

But with hindsight, it can be seen to make sense. The sun line at Saipan at the time she was radioing would have been 154-334. Exceedingly close! She was, according to such calculations, only a short distance south of the island.

And the radio-fading-out puzzle which baffled both Amelia and the Coast Guard cutter would be understandable when one considers where she was. Although her radio transmitter had a capability of 1000 miles, she was at that point of her communication pulling beyond that distance. She was soaring toward Saipan island, not Howland.

With her gas going fast, her radio losing contact

121

with the Coast Guard cutter, the last hours were upon her—and upon Fred Noonan.

The two fliers were in an area of mystery only a few Japanese fishermen were aware of—those who had marked the disappearance of fellow villagers in those uncertain waters.

Are Amelia Earhart—and her navigator—down there in the depths with them, beneath the Devil's Sea? Or was her craft affected by some strange electromagnetic force that "pulled" it from its goal? Perhaps, even, disintegrated it?

I guess the world will never tire of asking such questions or of hoping for some answers to them.

# Chapter 14

## ONE AGAINST THE TRIANGLE

It takes a lot of muscle, guts, and know-how to face the Triangle alone. Several men have tried. Some have made it. Some have not.

William Verity was one who made it. He did it alone in his hand-hewn 20-foot sailboat. Thomas Gatch had a dream of another kind. He wanted to make the first manned balloon crossing of the Atlantic. He vanished reaching for his dream. Benson Huggard tried for a swimming record. He did not reach his goal but lived to tell his story. Others, too, have had their share of solo adventure.

Bill Verity would not seem the type to man a balloon. His compact five-foot-eight frame carrying some 195 pounds of flesh and muscle belongs to the equally firmly constructed boats that argue against the angriest oceans. Bill Verity is a man who appears to have been born to fight the elements of earth. He can shout at the winds and curse the lightning—all with the assurance that he will win the battle.

He certainly won out on the voyage that took him through the deadly Bermuda Triangle in September of 1969.

Of strong Irish descent, Verity had long had an ambition to prove that America could have been discovered by an Irishman. Not long after his fortieth birthday, Bill Verity launched a bold plan. He would build a replica of the wooden boat of a legendary Irish monk named Brendan who is credited by folklore with having sailed across the Atlantic Ocean in the 6th century.

Crafting the boat by hand himself, Verity used the primitive tools of that early century and fashioned the type of boat known in that day. It took skill, time, and patience. But by the spring of 1969 he was done. He made detailed preparations for a solo voyage of 115 days to cross the wide Atlantic.

His journal for that trip starts with the simple entry:

May 22, 1969
Departed Fewit Peir, County Kerry 12:15
p.m. Towed to mouth of Tralee Bay and
underway at 1:50. Wind East 15 mph.

By September first, Brendan the Second had entered the Triangle. His arrival did not pass unnoticed by the elements! He was met by the fiercest lightning and thunder he had ever experienced. He recorded in his journal for September 4th:

Lightning! Lighting! And more lightning!—
Damn-Damn-Damn What a night!

Today Bill Verity can still recall the horror of those days and nights in the Triangle area. "I could smell the ozone—that metallic odor of spent electricity as the bolts hit the water. If ever a devil hung around anywhere, it's gotta be the Triangle. I swear you can smell the sulphur!" Bill says with a half-hidden smile.

Equally as discomforting as the lightning crashes and the thunder shatterings was the poorly operating radio. Bill noted on September 8:

". . . Radio reception poor the last two days. Never knew it to work so erratically! What the hell is wrong? Sun spots maybe? Is there something to this Triangle electro-magnetic force they talk about maybe?"

On the 9th, after several nights with no sleep, Bill dozed off in spite of the storm, the moldy bread, and his aching stomach, in spite of a crazy radio and no smell of land. In spite of all, he was too tired to work or worry. He stretched out in his hand-hewn boat, plummeting up and down the cascading waves, and closed his weary eyes.

He began to recall another time, alone on a solo sail when he had fallen fast asleep from exhaustion. An eerie experience he would never forget. In spite of the fact that he had been in a deep sleep, he awakened abruptly to the sound of his own name being called.

"Bill! Bill!" he heard distinctly.

He snapped awake in shock. Who in hell could be calling him way out in the middle of nowhere? He opened his eyes and discovered that his sailboat was headed straight for the rocks! Quickly he shifted sail and guided her away from a killing and unexpected landing!

Where had the voice come from?

"I don't know where the hell it came from—I only know I heard it and it saved my boat and probably my life!" Bill says.

Shades of the "mysterious Voice" heard by Francis Wagner on his many plane flights as described in Chapter 8, perhaps?

If you run into Bill Verity sometime—and that can be *anywhere*—he's always on the go—he can tell you about his Triangle trip (and don't believe the report in one of the books devoted to that subject that he disappeared in the mystery zone. He's very much still around. In fact at this writing he is in the South Seas replicating the longboat voyage of Captain Bligh after the mutiny of the *Bounty*!) Bill can tell you himself about the secret voice that saved his life.

All of which makes Bill Verity a specially fortunate (and skillful) adventurer.

Tom Gatch the balloonist did not survive to merit the same credentials.

From the detailed and careful plans made for the airflight over the Atlantic, a safe voyage seemed a fair assumption. Gatch himself had designed what he considered a foolproof vehicle of transport. The compact six-foot gondola was pronounced unsinkable. It was suspended from ten "super-pressure" helium balloons—a design often referred to as a "contraption" that, when assembled, stood 190 feet tall.

"Contraption" or no, one thing is sure, Tom Gatch was no tinhorn adventurer or fly-by-night kook. He was a respected, 48-year-old reserve colonel who was considered by his associates to be "level-headed" and "extremely disciplined." He was also known to be brave, a fact proved by a Bronze Star award for action in Korea.

But Tom had his private concerns and his inner urges. A quiet-spoken bachelor, fiercely dedicated to physical fitness, he was filled with creative talents. He was a novelist, a playwright, and a gentle hermit who craved and enjoyed solitude.

He was also a scholar of the universe. Fascinated with the forces of nature, he made a study of hurricanes, tornadoes, floods, earthquakes—how insignificant man was in the face of such powers! And what strength man might build for his world and himself if he could learn to harness these forces!

The possibility intrigued Tom Gatch.

Was that fascination with the forces of nature behind his solo trip plans? Was he thinking of that challenge when he slipped his lean frame into the spherical gondola he dubbed *Light Heart* on February 18th, 1974? Did he carry in his heart, as he floated upwards with those ten helium balloons, the lofty desire to aid his fellow man with a powerful discovery?

*Light Heart* swept airily away from the field at Harrisburg, Pennsylvania, that cold February day, headed eastward. No one, not even Gatch himself, had any real idea as to where the balloons would take him. He might come down in Europe. Africa, perhaps. At any rate, Tom was prepared. He carried with him on board the flags of a dozen countries. He was well-equipped to honor the landing site of the first manned balloon crossing of the Atlantic Ocean.

Today the flags lie lost somewhere with Tom and his airy "contraption." Though he was well-equipped with excellent radio apparatus as well as a compass, altimeter, parachute, and an inflatable life raft, not one of those lifesaving objects has ever been spotted, nor a trace of the balloonist himself.

His course took him over the Triangle. His balloon was reported by one witness as being seen southwest of the Azores. No evidence has ever been found of the brave and very lost Tom Gatch who may have struck the greatest adventure of all time— an aerial flight through space—and, perhaps, even time?

Benson Huggard's venture was different from that of a solo sailor or a lone balloonist. His Triangle attempt was from *within* the water. He challenged the Devil's deeps by planning what he called "The Swim of the Century." It was a 165-mile marathon from the Florida Keys to Freeport in the Bahamas! He would swim it nude (and with the well-thought-out protection of technology) within the framework of a "shark cage" which would be towed by a 40-foot yacht.

At 1:20 p.m. on May 22, 1975, Benson plunged into the warm waters of the Gulf Stream off Florida.

"Don't pull me out unless I'm dead," he said.

Twenty-nine hours and twenty-five minutes later, not quite dead, Huggard was pulled out of the Atlantic just south of Bimini. Though he hadn't made his goal to Freeport, he did make a new record as far as the Swimming Hall of Fame is concerned.

But the swim had run into dreadful problems— chiefly from the water itself. When, in the darkness of the night, Huggard looked down into the depths, in the light of the high intensity underwater light mounted on the front end of the cage, he could see "dark, menacing shapes," some of them six and seven feet long, nosing at the wire cage, occasionally thumping against the aluminum wiring.

By dawn Huggard was still swimming but the cage had sunk and now the ocean water was pouring over the cage bringing with it a Portuguese man-of-war that stung Huggard on his hands and feet. Then came the problems with jellyfish. His mouth became so swollen he could hardly eat. Finally, he was over the edge of the fast-sinking cage, violently sick to his stomach.

By 6:15 that evening, the cage was obviously doomed—and so, it seemed, was Huggard. They pulled him from the water. Groaning his disappointment, Benson Huggard protested, "I could have made it!"

Later his trainer was asked what had happened to the shark cage.

His reply was simple.

"The Bermuda Triangle tore it apart!"

One loner who made it through the Triangle was not a sailor, a balloonist, or a swimmer. He was a pilot. Jim Blocker, a corporate pilot from Atlanta, Georgia, had a bizarre experience that was reported in the *National Enquirer* of July 15th, 1975. It occurred in February of 1968. He told the newspaper:

"I took off in clear weather in the Triangle from Nassau headed for Palm Beach, Florida. I filed a flight plan for 8000 feet but the control tower recommended that I change to 6000 feet because two other planes flying at 8000 feet had disappeared without a trace on that same day!

"Well, about 40 miles north of Nassau, my radio suddenly went dead. Then my compass started spinning crazily and all my navigational aids stopped working—even my very-high-frequency directional finder, which is unheard of.

"Finally, I came out of the clouds—and wow! Where was I? I was 150 miles northeast of Nassau . . . and I had been heading *northwest!*"

Jim Blocker still shakes his head over that eerie experience.

"I have no doubt in the world that there's some strange force at work in the Triangle—probably a powerful electromagnetic field," he says.

Probably every adventurer who ever dared the Devil's Triangle would agree with him.

# Chapter 15

## THE PSYCHIC PROBERS

The psychics of the world have done their share of adventuring into the terrors of the Triangle.

In my *Bermuda Triangle* book I made mention in the final chapter, which examined possible explanations of the mystery area, of a Connecticut psychic named Ed Snedeker. Mr. Snedeker declares he has frequently been in touch with the vanished people from this baffling region. They were "picked up" or "sucked up" by atmospheric "sleeves"—a type of funnel phenomenon invisible to the human eye—which whirls its prey in a course from north to south, finally depositing its contents, both human and inert, in the vicinity of the Antarctic or, frequently, *beyond*.

One "voice" Mr. Snedeker heard came to him from someplace down within the hollow of the earth! It belonged to an RAF pilot, says the psychic, who vanished in the Bermuda Triangle around 1945.

Ed Snedeker is not alone in the "funnel theory." A similar solution has been proposed by an ESP expert, Norman Slater, of Kenosha, Winconsin. Mr. Slater will tell you he has uncovered three danger traps in the Triangle. He calls them "hot spots." They exist within a three-mile radius off the Florida coast. Any ship or plane that might be in the vicinity would be sucked down into the bowels of the Gulf Stream in these zones and deposited in a time machine. This time mechanism exists in the form of a funnel which holds the victims in an invisible dimension until it releases them . . . backwards or forward in time.

It's a short step in the psychic world from a funnel that sucks up victims to a pyramid power that acts like a magnet and draws planes and people down into the ocean depths.

One proponent of the pyramid theory is the noted trance medium, Dr. Joseph Jeffers of St. James, Missouri.

In an interview with *National Insider* newspaperman Tom Earnest, recently, Dr. Jeffers explained his solution of the Triangle mystery. The information, he stated, came to him and several of his followers while in meditation with Yahweh, creator of the universe.

"Yahweh told us the legend of Atlantis is true, that the continent did exist and that the remains of this sunken continent are instrumental in causing the strange happenings in the Bermuda Triangle.

". . . at one time . . . Atlantis was a perfect world, a paradise. There was no sickness, disease, or even death. The people lived in harmony under the creator, Yahweh.

"They had machines, including aircraft, which were more sophisticated than those we have today ...

"Atlanteans destroyed their own world when hatred grew into war and they withdrew from Yahweh and thought they could do without him."

The consequence? The destruction of Atlantis.

But not quite *all* of Atlantis.

The force behind the energy used by Atlanteans in their super-sophisticated civilization was a huge pyramid, miles in diameter.

"This pyramid," Jeffers told *Insider,* "received its power from the cosmos of the universe and from Orion, Yahweh's headquarters. As the people turned away from the creator, thinking the power of the pyramid would be all they needed, the continent began to break up and sink.

"As the continent sank, this powerful pyramid also sank very deeply into a large crater in the ocean floor. It remains hidden there today."

The force from this buried pyramid is so powerful, declares Jeffers, the human body burns up or disintegrates before the ship or plane enters the suction.

What activates the pyramid force?

"Atmospheric conditions," said Dr. Jeffers, "including static electricity, radiation, and sun spots, as well as the particular rotation of the earth in relation to other points in the universe ... these all work to trigger the Triangle."

Another top psychic in our country, Page Bryant of Tampa, Florida, goes for the unknown energy force "stationed", so to speak, in the Triangle also. In an interview with James Paul Chaplin for the *Na-*

*tional Tattler* newspaper of January 26, 1975, Mrs. Bryant declared that an unknown energy force dematerializes aircraft and ships in the mystery zone and, acts, as well, as a "channel" through which UFO's may enter and exit from earth.

Page Bryant does not do her exploration through thought waves alone; she personally flew the Triangle twice, piloted by Bob Burr.

The first time was traumatic. On July 20 1974, the seeress, accompanied by a witness, Cynthia Stanley, boarded a Cessna 172 at St. Petersburg. The craft took off for West Palm Beach, then out over the Atlantic to the Bahamas, then down to Walker Cay and finally, back again over the Bahamas headed for Miami.

The weather was perfect. Bob Burr found no difficulties in flying whatsoever. But over the Bahamas the first time, Mrs. Bryant slipped into a deep trance which lasted for half an hour.

In her "sleep" state, the seeress was no longer in a Cessna 172 but in a large military plane zooming speedily toward storm clouds ahead. In the next instant, Mrs. Bryant felt herself in still another airplane—a small private craft. It also was headed for storm clouds.

"The thunder rumbled louder than the plane's engine, and I knew I was caught up in a terrible storm. I was unable to maintain my bearings. The compass wouldn't function. I had no way of telling which way I was headed. I couldn't even tell the water from the sky. I was lost. Blackness was all around me.

"Then, suddenly, I became aware of brilliant flashes of yellow-gold lightning, which were extremely strong. My plane was being violently tossed about. I frantically tried to radio, 'Mayday! Mayday!' but there was no reply.

"I tried to struggle to regain control of the plane and maneuver it through an opening in the clouds. The opening had taken on the appearance of a slit, something like a light shining under a door.

"Just then the plane was uncontrollably turned sideways and was being sucked through the opening. At the same time I felt immense pressure crushing my chest. I felt as though I was being forced out through my breaking skin—blown apart and flattened—as the plane entered the white slit in the sky. . . .

When Mrs. Bryant snapped out of her trance, she was crying and felt sick to her stomach.

"I have never been so frightened as I was just before coming out of trance that day," she recalled to the reporter later.

A short time after this traumatic flight, Mrs. Bryant underwent hypnosis to see what might be uncovered. A former Arizona resident, hypnotist Al Miner of St. Petersburg, gave her several sessions, which all added up to reveal what Mrs. Bryant felt was startling information: the Bermuda Triangle is the vortex of an unknown energy field that draws its power from other planets as well as from the magnetic field of the earth.

Page Bryant will tell you that man's instruments cannot as yet detect this field, but will achieve such capability by 1983. This energy field, she asserts, is used by UFO's to enter and exit from earth's atmosphere.

"I don't feel there is an actual triangle involved in this phenomena. It's actually a 'tube' of energy that extends through the earth shooting out through the section of the Atlantic we call the Bermuda Triangle and has a corresponding sector in the Pacific south of Japan called the 'Devil's Sea' where ships have also disappeared under mysterious circumstances.

"Perhaps a few sea and air craft have been taken up by UFO's for scientific research, but the majority of those lost ships have vanished because they flew or sailed directly into the heart of this energy beam . . .

"What actually happens to those who disappear is that they dematerialize, pass on into another dimension. They're dead to us on this plane, but their energies, their spirits, go on. I know because on that first flight I made over the Triangle, I made transmedium contact with one of the gunners who disappeared December 5, 1945. His name is Robert Francis Gallivan. During one of my hypnosis sessions, he told me: 'My God, let me tell what happened!' "

UFO's and a hidden city beneath the earth's surface form a major basis for explaining the phenomenon of the Bermuda Triangle to several psychics.

An Indonesian prophetess by the name of Farida is one such seeress. Her information seems to be pretty direct. She got it, she claims, from space beings themselves who have recruited her as their ambassador. She is under orders to board a UFO on a Puerto Rican beach in the near future and ride it to a city beneath the earth's surface.

How did Farida come by such a conviction?

According to an interview recently in the *National Insider,* April 27, 1975, it all began a few years ago in February when the Indonesian prophetess was visiting in the Mojave Desert of Southern California. One night as she was admiring the clear, crystal-starred heavens above her, she caught sight of a "really beautiful" flying saucer. It descended toward her, and before she knew it she was being approached by "space beings."

"Go to the Bermuda Triangle," they ordered in no uncertain terms. "Go to the beach of Puerto Rico where you will be met by a flying saucer. It will take you beneath the earth to a place where thousands of ships, airplanes, and people who have vanished in the Triangle are now living comfortably."

She is now training "like an astronaut," the seeress informed the reporter. "If I make one mistake, I can die."

Believing there are twelve Triangles around the globe, Farida states the conviction that all the people who have ever vanished in any of them all now live inside the earth.

"I believe I can bring some of them out, if they want to come out", she asserted, adding quickly, ". . . that. is, if I come out."

Farida may choose not to come out. "If it is beautiful inside, maybe I'll remain."

"But," the prophetess makes it clear, "if I am to come out, I have to know the key (to the Triangle)."

Not claiming to know all the answers, Farida does admit she feels the lost continent of Atlantis has something to do with the disappearances. Her main aim at this point is to go to inner earth, learn the solution to the mystery, and return with the information.

Included in Farida's plans prior to her Triangle mission is a visit to Washington to talk to President Ford and Vice President Rockefeller to fill them in on the worth of her investigation.

If it all ends up that she never returns from the inner earth voyage, Farida will not be concerned.

"I shall be content to live with the others in the Fourth Dimension," she states coolly.

Not so calm about the prospects of a "no return," a planned voyage of psychics into the Bermuda Triangle for June 27th, 1975, was cancelled at the last moment. Too many of the psychics scheduled for the expedition had been receiving "negative impressions.'"

First plans for such a psychic investigation of the mystery zone were revealed in late '74. *Newsweek* magazine made note of it in an article devoted to the unsolved peculiarities of the Triangle called "Graveyard of the Atlantic." In summing up several of the suggested solutions, the magazine concluded with:

"To test such theories, a parapsychological institute called the Isis Center for Research and Study of the Esoteric Arts, based in Silver Spring, Maryland, is planning to take 300 psychics and scientists on a cruise into the Triangle next June. The researchers hope to make contact with whatever 'higher intelligences' may lurk under the sea. A similar expedition into the Devil's Sea was made by a group of Japanese scientists in 1955. Nothing has been heard of them since."

Six months after that article appeared, a communication was sent to all media by the Isis Center. It read, in part:

"The Isis Center announced today cancellation of its planned trip to the Bermuda Triangle. Scheduled to leave New York City June 27th, the trip was designed to explore the mysteries of the Bermuda Triangle region with special emphasis on the effects of the Triangle on psychic abilities . . .

"Acccording to Jean Byrd, President of the Isis Center, a number of the psychics scheduled to go began in May to receive impressions, dreams, and feelings of a negative nature about the outcome of the trip. By late May, these had increased in negativity to the point that the psychics asked to withdraw from participation in the cruise. Without the psychics, the goals and objectives of the Isis research program could not be met, and the decision to cancel was made.

"The Bermuda triangle has a long history of unexplained disasters, and many investigators of the region have met with disappointments, unusual events, and even loss of life in connection with their investigation of the area. In February, 1975, a Florida-based group planned a cruise to the area involving psychics and scientists, but this trip, too, failed to materialize . . ."

The news release went on to say that in the spring of 1976, Hermes International Communications Institute, based in Newport, Rhode Island, hopes to sponsor a cruise to the Bermuda Triangle.

Investigative cruises, psychic as well as scientific, are increasing month by month. It would seem America may be short on conclusive answers to an age-old mystery, but not on courage to find them.

# Chapter 16

## THEY'RE NOT TALKING!

Not all travelers in the Triangle are as willing—or able, perhaps I should say—to talk about their experiences as the foregoing lone sailors, yachtsmen and skin divers. I have found innumerable commercial pilots, charter boat captains, military personnel, etc., who hesitate to speak their minds for fear of professional criticism. If they do talk, it's with the understanding they will not be quoted by name.

Then there are others, I have learned, who fall into a sort of superstitious class. They don't want to talk about something they don't want to believe. But their fear is so real they carry amulets in their cockpits or on their persons.

As one former professional flyer put it in an interview recently, "Pilots don't want to believe there's anything out there. They're afraid to. They don't even want to talk about it."

On the whole, pilots are a stable breed, no-nonsense men. They are trained to count on instruments, not on their senses. They give the Triangle Mystery short shrift, except for an occasional flyer who finds his instruments behaving erratically and suddenly can't count on them!

One such pilot who flies an air-taxi service from Florida to several islands in the Triangle acknowledges that he has had several unnerving experiences with haywire instruments, particularly over North Andros. He has found his magnetic compass will spin, his directional finder will not indicate the location of the air station, and his radio willl suddenly go dead. Such zones of "deadliness" are quite commonly experienced by pilots and mariners, I learned, especially in the Bahamas.

Officials of airlines, shipping companies, and the military, of course, stand shoulder to shoulder against all Triangle talk. As one Coast Guard spokesman put it, "Sheer bull. The fact is that too many dingalings buy a new boat, take a bunch of friends over to Bimini for the weekend, and find they can't handle one of the freak storms that come up out there. Before you know it, we got another missing boat on our hands. We average over twenty calls a day in a year's time. But it's not due to anything supernatural. That's a lot of bull."

The Coast Guard recently put out a set of official statements for its men to refer to in handling the ever-increasing number of inquiries pouring in from the public, the press, and researchers.

Such a reference constitutes an official standpoint.

Unofficial is something else again.

Off the record, the military, like everyone else, hash and rehash the Triangle puzzle. And many a strange incident comes into discussion. I was told about one such occasion by a Coast Guardsman attached to the Coast Guard cutter *Pontchartrain*.

Early in 1973 the ship was assigned to Ocean Station Echo, a position in the Atlantic Ocean about 800 miles east of Bermuda. At that time, Coast Guard ships were stationed at posts far out at sea to keep aircraft flying between the United States and Europe informed in the event of a position check. The custom is now obsolete. But in those days the patrols spent long weeks at their sea stations . . . some forty days at a stretch.

En route to the station nothing unusual occurred. But a few days after arrival at Echo position the cutter received a Mayday on the emergency frequency.

Immediately the crew went into action, chasing the signals. To their amazement, the signals went under and disappeared!

The cutter returned to Echo position only to pick up once again a Mayday on the emergency frequency. Once more they set out following the SOS signals and, as before, were flabbergasted to find them disappearing again.

This happened time after time while the *Pontchartrain* was at Echo. Not once could they locate any distressed vessel or whatever it was. Finally, on a chase for the SOS signal some time later, the cutter broke off the hunt because of low fuel. It headed for an oceanographic standard section tract located about 400 miles off the North Carolina coast.

Prior to arrival at the first section of the tract, weather and sea conditions were relatively calm. But soon after the first seawater sample bottle was submerged, the weather took an abrupt change. Howling winds and building seas made constant maneuvering of the ship necessary in order to retrieve the cast. With the samples finally aboard, the ship steamed en route to the next position along the tract. The winds and water had by now built to such intensity that the ship's arrival at position was delayed.

When it did make the destination, conditions were so severe only two of a 13-bottle cast were lowered because it was obvious it would be impossible to retrieve the samples. The ship radioed for and received permission to abort and head for home.

The cutter turned at Wilmington, North Carolina, for home port at Norfolk, Virginia. Then a remarkable thing was discovered: the ship in her homeward course was on a heading with the wind and seas dead astern!

The young Coastguardsman shook his head as he concluded his story.

"It was as if some force other than the weather elements was pushing us out of the area. It was the weirdest feeling any of us had ever experienced! None of us will ever forget that trip and, boy, were we glad to get back home!"

Commercial pilots report their share of startling experiences, too. One captain of a major airline that flies from Washington to Bermuda told me of repeated problems he and other pilots have found in the Triangle with the plane's gyroscope. Even though the stabilizing mechanism is handled electronically, it won't operate properly in the Triangle zone! In a certain area en route to Bermuda the right wing dips every trip and has to be counteracted by pilot control!

One of the most silent of the Triangle daredevils is a man in Key Largo, Florida, who knows the waters of his area as well as the features on his own rugged face. He knows the surface sea and its depths as well, as he has spent a large portion of his life searching for some of the lost treasure that lies under the green tides of the Caribbean.

As any dedicated treasure hunter can tell you, the Caribbean is a storehouse of buried wealth. All through the 1500s, the 1600s and well into the 1700s, Spain was exploiting her rich holdings in the New World. Her laden galleons converged at Havana after having filled up with gold, silver, and other valuables and together proceeded north in an armada for protection against pirates. The treasure fleet would ride the Gulf Stream north and then at Cape Hatteras would veer out eastward across the Atlantic.

Such voyages were ravaged by marauders or hurricanes, or both, leaving a large percentage of many an armada plunging into the ocean depths. To this day, hundreds of such ill-fated vessels lie buried in the sands of the Caribbean.

One of these ships was an ecstatic surprise for a Key Largo treasure seeker. One beautiful day after years of intensive search, the diver found the wreck he'd so long sought. The thought of what riches lay ahead was mind-staggering. Finds on such wrecks have netted millions of dollars not only in intrinsic value of the silver and gold but in historical worth as well in the case of rare artifacts.

Friends of the treasure hunter noted the gleam of

joy in the man's face the day he located the wreck. Excitement ran through those who shared his confidence.

Then, the diver went out alone for a re-check before making salvaging plans. When he came back, as one local man put it, "He was a changed man." He would not speak of the find again. He never went out after it again. Nothing would he say to explain his new indifference.

"Somethin' happened to him out there that last time. Somethin' that scared the wits out of him. I know the man, and it's plain somethin' happened," a Key Largo man confided to me. "But I guess we'll never know what. He'll never say . . ."

The treasure hunter joins the ranks of many who have dared the Triangle and come back but will not talk about it.

One more bafflement to add to what is already surely the world's greatest puzzle.

# Chapter 17

## THE DISAPPEARING, REAPPEARING, DISAPPEARING CYCLOPS

Of all the strange incidents that have occurred in the Triangle zone, dating back nearly five centuries to the voyage of Columbus, probably the single most baffling one—and the most startling one by reason of its sheer magnitude—was the vanishing of the huge Navy collier, *Cyclops,* in 1918.

That disappearance was the biggest attention-getter of all the many craft that had been subtly and without too much fanfare quietly disappearing off the face of the sea.

In the early years of this country's navigational history, when a craft didn't put in an appearance as scheduled, it was accepted as just another tragic and unhappy incident, because ships were frequently waylaid or sunk, and the causes varied from hurricanes to pirates. But in the opening years of the twentieth century when ship-to-shore radio came into use, a new look at the situation slowly evolved. Why were no emergency messages received? Why no debris? Why no bodies?

Toward the middle of the month of March in 1918 newspapers all over America printed the astounding announcement that an American naval collier was lost—lost without a trace or any signal of distress whatever. She had simply vanished in a voyage homeward bound from Barbados to Norfolk, Virginia.

As the local newspaper put it—the *Virginian-Pilot*—the *Cyclops*'s "FATE MAY BE ANOTHER MYSTERY OF THE SEA."

So it was—and is.

The Navy collier was a stupendous loss and surely did more than any previous vanishing to bolster the ever-growing legend that this portion of the Atlantic was, indeed, as the 16th-century navigators had dubbed it, a "Region of the Devils." Something strange, it was suspected, did "haunt" the area. Something so powerful it could do away with a gigantic supply ship with some 300 persons aboard!

The *Cyclops* was a giant in its day. Its weight was 19,000 tons, its length about the equivalent of two football fields, measured end to end! It was capable of making more than fourteen knots and it was manned by an experienced crew of 236 officers and men. On this particular voyage, the ship also carried an interesting roster of passengers: the U.S. consul general to Brazil; two AWOL Marines and three seamen being returned to the States to stand trial for murder. A strange assortment.

Did the accused murderers have anything to do with the disappearance? Was the presence of the

147

consul general related to it in any way? He was accused of being pro-German. Since World War I was still going on, had he earlier arranged to turn the ship over to the enemy? Or had the captain himself surrendered his ship? Captain Worley had been born in Germany.

Did a German sub sink the vessel? Did the collier's cargo explode? It was carrying manganese dioxide, frequently highly explosive. Or, most simply of all, had the ship capsized in a storm?

Each of the foregoing questions was scrutinized—and proved invalid.

After the war, the German naval archives were examined for some answer to the mystery. There was none. No report of a sub torpedoing the *Cyclops*; no mention of any "deal" to turn over the ship to the Germans by the captain or any crew member or passenger.

Neither was the explosion theory acceptable, as even in the most violent holocausts, debris is left behind. Neither was there any evidence of a storm along the *Cyclops*'s route at the time of her voyage. High winds periodically but nothing a vessel of her type couldn't have handled.

No matter what angle the investigation pursued, the results were baffling. There was no solution. It still stands today as one of the outstanding puzzles of the Triangle zone. The great *Cyclops* was the first large radio-equipped vessel to vanish without a hint of trouble. It had never sent a single SOS. Without a word, it vanished for all time without leaving a clue.

Or did it?

In 1968 an interesting thing occurred. A Navy diver, Dean Hawes, searching beneath the waters about 70 miles east of Norfolk in the Atlantic Ocean for the lost submarine, *Scorpion,* came upon a long-buried wreck. The old ship had an unusually high bridge, supported by steel uprights. Hawes had never seen anything like it. Before he could investigate the sunken craft, however, he was forced to surface. Then rough weather forced him to abandon the project entirely.

But Hawes was intrigued by his discovery. Something gave him an inner conviction he had come upon the long-vanished naval collier. Searching out a photograph of the famous ship, he was delighted to find it strongly resembled his find. The bridge was high above the deck just as that of his sunken craft had been!

However, Hawes was never able to re-locate the vessel in its watery grave. He pursued, coaxing interest out of Virginia Representative G. William Whitehurst, who in turn got the Navy to agree to investigate. Subsequently, Navy divers combed the area as a training exercise in an effort to re-locate the aged ship reported by Hawes. Nothing was found.

Six years later in August of 1974, two scuba divers reported a find in the same area. Navy Commander Lucio Hill of Virginia Beach and Bill Edelstein of Norfolk suspected they, too, might have come upon the aged collier. They and six other members of a diving club poked around the wreck that rested some 190 feet below the Atlantic some 70 miles northeast of Cape Charles.

But their search revealed a ship of an entirely different design from that described by Hawes. This vessel was of a World War II cargo type and bore the scar of an apparent collision. A 30-foot gash ripped downward from the main deck to the waterline on the starboard side just forward of the bridge. The ship's lifeboat davits were swung out; the lifeboats were gone, and there was no indication that any person had gone down with the ship. The divers, who descended in groups of four, reported finding radar, an electronic navigation aid which was not invented until the 1930s—long after the disappearance of the World War I *Cyclops*.

Following the divers' expedition, the Navy salvage ship *Opportune* arrived on the scene. Whatever it pulled from the sunken vessel by way of salvage, one thing is certain, none of the items bore the name *Cyclops*.

Dean Hawes shrugs off the find. Examining the photos taken by the underwater cameras of the recent probers, he declares they bear no resemblance to the ship he discovered. He still feels convinced he was aboard the mysterious *Cyclops*—almost precisely fifty years after its last fatal voyage—an adventurer from today gazing upon a famous hulk from the past.

Whether or not the former Navy diver did indeed find the long-vanished collier, we cannot know. As it stands today, the old *Cyclops* still hides its history behind the veil of the Unknown which drops periodically over the mysterious Bermuda Triangle.

# Chapter 18

## TRIANGLE TROUBLES GO ON . . .

Periodically, Triangle troubles surface to the attention. Some old. Some new. One learns that such notables as Arthur Godfrey experienced them. Once a thorough debunker in the Triangle controversy, pilot Godfrey retracted his skepticism on a Dick Cavett Show in the early 1970s. He reported a nerve-shattering "close call" a short time before.

Godfrey, an experienced pilot, had been scheduled to go on the flight of a large experimental plane out of Hawaii. The plane was called the *Mars*. Anticipating the adventure, the showman made arrangements to arrive at the Hawaiian airport in good time. However, unpredictable events delayed his plane and the newly developed flying boat lifted off the airbase without its anticipated guest of honor. It was one of the most fortunate things that ever happened to Arthur Godfrey!

The veteran airman watched the flight on radar with a personal interest, every inch of him hankering to be on the craft. Suddenly, his heart nearly leaped out of his body when he saw the plane bleep utterly disappear off the screen right before his eyes.

"Poof!" exclaimed Godfrey as he recounted the incident for Cavett with a snap of his fingers. "She was there one moment—and I tell you, gone the next!" He added as the audience listened in hushed silence, "And they never found a *thing!* Not even a trace of an oil slick!"

Mysteries abound in the Pacific area. In November of 1967 one of the strangest marine inexplicables took place off Japan. Shortly before dawn, local radio towers received a distress signal from a ship identifying itself as the 10,626-ton U.S. tanker *Cleveland*. It reported it was on fire in the Western Pacific with 37 men aboard. The message detailed that the ship's engine room was afire and the tanker was taking water.

Rough seas and limited visibility hampered an air-sea search for the ship. The next afternoon, an oil slick was spotted off Sasebo, but no sign or trace of a tanker could be found. No remnant of life preserver equipment or remains of a single body or clothing. Strangest of all, when the Maritime Safety Agency of Japan contacted the ship's brokers, the Cleveland Transport Company of New York, the company declared the ship could not be where she was reported to have been. The brokers had received a report from its tanker; she was in Bombay, India.

Wherever she was, she was no longer on the face

of this earth. The Devil's Sea, it can be presumed, had taken another toll.

The year 1973 was an interesting one for the Bermuda Triangle.

In June a United Airlines 727 jet took off from Cleveland, landed at Atlanta, then jetted skyward headed for Miami International Airport. Making contact with Miami shortly after 10 p.m. the jet zoomed in on the 8000-foot lighted runway and made a perfect landing.

But a surprise awaited the crew and the passengers.

There was no terminal. No baggage carriers or United employees were there to meet them.

Much to the chagrin of the pilot and co-pilot, they found they were not at Miami but at Opa-Locka Airfield of Florida's Coast Guard Air Search and Rescue Station (the very unit that had been called into action many years before in the now famous search for the five lost Avenger planes at the close of World War II, probably the Triangle's most famous case).

The Opa-Locka field was eight miles north on the Florida coastline from Miami. The craft's calculations went awry; confusion as to direction occurred once again, as is so frequently the case in the Triangle environs. Fortunately, unlike the earlier disorientation of the Avenger pilots, the United airliner landed with not a single problem—except how they would ever explain to the Federal Aviation Administration their arriving at the wrong airport!

Opa-Locka itself was not a little surprised, either. "We don't normally see anything that large," declared one duty officer at the field, "but we handled it."

Very frequently, however, even the largest of ocean liners seem unable to cope with problems in the Triangle waters. In spite of all modern-day equipment, in recent years two big liners had to SOS for help. In September of 1973 the new Russian luxury ship, the M.S. *Mikhail Lermontov,* plying the Atlantic waters between Russia and the United States, made a special voyage from Manhattan to Bermuda. She rammed onto a reef so suddenly and unexpectedly that she was stuck fast, and she radioed for help. My husband and I were in a plane at the time which circled the distressed vessel. We were amazed such a thing could happen in our time.

A year and a half later, in April of 1974, another queen of the seas met trouble in the Triangle, the Cunard liner, R.M.S. *Queen Elizabeth 2.* All three of the *Queen*'s boilers failed, leaving the ship helpless about 187 miles southwest of Bermuda, right in the heart of the mystery zone.

The explanation was logical, yet illogical. An oil line ruptured, allowing oil to enter the boiler feed water, causing a boiler shutdown—a situation that immobilized the vessel. But that such an event could occur in this day and age is itself a staggering mystery. What happened to the backup system?

One puzzled scientist, among many, who saw it that way was a passenger on board the *QE 2,* Kramer J. Schatzlein, an engineer from Allentown, Pennsylvania. Kramer and his wife were on a Bermuda-bound vacation when the startling incident occurrred.

"It seemed incredible," Schatzlein told me, "that such a thing could occur on a ship like the *Elizabeth*! There must have been safeguards to prevent such a catastrophe! What happened to them?"

Other engineers have expressed the same amazement to me. I was unable to unearth a single other instance in which such an incident had occurred. I did uncover some tales that the *QE 2* had disappeared off the radar screen of a Coast Guard cutter that was following in her wake at the time of the breakdown. The Coast Guard states there is no record of any such observation in its files.

After 72 hours adrift, the *Queen*'s passengers were finally rescued by the Norwegian cruise ship, *Sea Venture,* and taken to Hamilton, Bermuda, where the tired and anxious adventurers were given hotel accommodations and showers (the first in three days). Eventually, the cruisers were returned to New York City.

Luckier than many forerunners they were, too. Passengers on such very early voyages as that of the good ship *Anne* did not fare so well. A stout vessel of 200 tons, she took off from Beaufort Town, Georgia Colony, in 1733 bearing colonists back to England. She set sail with a fair wind bearing her seawards. Nothing was ever heard from her again. She utterly vanished, and with her every soul on board, none of whom survived to tell the tale.

Thirty-three years later, during the peak of the Revolutionary War years, one of the signers of the daring Declaration of Independence, one Thomas Lynch of South Carolina, set sail from Charleston bound for a warmer climate. He had been ailing for some time and now that he'd aided in launching a new course of freedom for the American colonies he was going to find some much needed personal freedom and rest in the southern climes until his strength returned. His ship lifted canvas to the winds on a perfectly beautiful day in the year 1779. It glided out of Charleston harbor and bent toward the distant horizon. Neither he, nor the ship, nor anyone else on board was ever seen or heard of again.

Thirty-three years later (is there any significance in this same interval of time?), a swift packet ship departed Georgetown port, a short distance up the coast from Charleston, bearing the state's First Lady, Governor Alston's beautiful wife, Theodosia Burr Alston, northward to meet her father, Aaron Burr, recently returned from European exile. Mr. Burr walked the Battery of New York City's harbor in vain—for weeks. His daughter never arrived. The mystery of what might have happened perplexes to this day. I covered the details of that incident in my *Bermuda Triangle*.

There are no survivors, either, from one of the Triangle's more recent tragedies, the disappearance of a $300,000 corporation yacht, the *Saba Bank* in 1974.

The time was April, a period when tropical waters are usually at their best. The skies were clear and the winds moderate. The *Saba Bank* pulled out of Nassau in the Bahamas headed for Miami some 150 nautical miles away by the most direct route. But the *Saba* crew had not specified to anyone what exact course they proposed to take. They left Nassau on March 10th due to reach Miami on April 8th. They never arrived.

The 54-foot yacht was scheduled to go into charter service. Owned by Vasco Corporation of Wilmington, Delaware, it was on its shakedown cruise skippered by four experienced seamen. The boat was equipped with every safety device imaginable. It had radar, single sideband and VHF radio, inflatable, self-releasing life rafts, a Boston whaler with an outboard motor as well as a complete line of emergency gear including distress flares.

The Coast Guard conducted an intensive search for several weeks. The Bahamas Coast Guard aided in the tracking. When not a sign or a clue was forthcoming by the 24th of the month, the search was abandoned. Not a trace of the vanished yacht has been found to this day, although both Vasco Corporation and Lloyd's of London have offered substantial rewards for information which still stand to this moment.

As with all the other Triangle disappearances, the loss of the *Saba Bank* seems unbelievable. A business partner of one of the vanished seamen, John Tarquino of Vineland, New Jersey, is Edward Rone. In an interview with the *Philadelphia Bulletin* of April 26, 1974, Rone stated the absolute conviction the missing yacht would be found. It had to be safe, he declared, for she had "all the latest equipment, including lifeboats and radios capable of broadcasting 2000 miles."

Equipment or no equipment, not a word was ever heard from the corporation yacht. Its stalwart structure and its crew of four (Cy Zentner and Eliott Cohen, both of Philadelphia, and Raphael Kaplan and John Tarquino of South Jersey) all stepped into the Triangle's mysterious heart, like so many predecessors, never to be heard from again.

# Chapter 19

## BLACK HOLES AND OTHER COSMIC DOINGS

The most meaningful clues as to what might be affecting the Triangle zone may point to factors so large and awesome, indeed so catastrophic, that man overlooks them from the sheer enormity of their significance.

Such phenomena as magnetic pole reversal, for one.

It is theorized that periodically over long eons of time, the magnetic field that envelops the earth gradually diminishes, then fades almost altogether. Then it returns, growing back to full strength but with one great resultant change: the negative and positive poles are reversed!

According to an article in *Time* magazine not so long ago, such changes are accompanied by perceptible differences in earth's weather patterns and even in animal life. As one example, a reversal of the magnetic poles which took place between 60 and 70 million years ago coincided with the disappearance of the great lizards from the face of our planet, leaving man room to develop and become the dominant species.

Scientific reasoning suggests that the magnetic poles reverse approximately every 220,000 years. But the last reversal occurred about 700,000 years ago, leaving us with a literally earth-shaking event some 480,000 years overdue!

Are the magnetic peculiarities reported in the Triangle evidence related somehow to this pending catastrophe? A kind of forewarning? Certainly, though we can't know the detailed effects of such an event, we can be sure it would upset our compasses and navigational instruments, to say the very least. Perhaps it would be a catastrophe so cataclysmic "it isn't worth anyone's worrying about," as one scientist recently expressed it.

Surely, black holes in space fall into that same category.

Discussing a phenomenon of the scope of black holes is not easy but understanding a little may go a long way in explaining the triangle puzzle.

Einstein told the world that our universe was held together by the heavy pull of the magnetic bodies within it. But scientists have been unable to locate more than two percent of that necessary mass—until the black hole theory.

That theory concerns the life cycle of very old stars which have exploded all their nuclear fuel and are collapsing inward—or imploding. A neutron star is such a star. In its dying state, giving off gasps of nuclear fuel, it throws off pieces of its mass and it becomes a "nova." Such a star is the well-known "Crab Nebula" which is actually the shell of an ancient star whose explosion was noted by the Chinese in the year 1045.

The nova, then, is able to continue "living" by the balanced process of retaining enough of the radiation from the remains of fuel in its core to balance the implosion rate of its reduced size. In this way it goes on existing in a peaceful state of old age.

But not all stars age so gracefully.

If the star is heavier than the sun—so extremely heavy that it cannot "shake off" material fast enough to retain such a balance, it collapses into such a heavy mass of crushed atoms of matter that a *cubic inch* of material weighs *trillions of tons*.

Nothing can escape such tremendous gravity pull —not even light—with the result that the star becomes invisible—a black hole in space.

The most awesome and mind-boggling aspect of the black hole is the fact that anything sucked into the black hole would travel at tremendous speed, exceeding that of light—a situation in which mass becomes infinite and time ceases to exist. Theoretically, anything drawn into a black hole would emerge in another universe or dimension!

Has there ever been any relationship between the presence of Black Holes in space and the area of the Bermuda Triangle?

Perhaps an event which occurred June 30th, 1908, is significant.

The place was Siberia, the time early morning.

Villagers going about their early morning duties in the wide wastes of the barren stretches noticed a fantastic thing—a huge fireball in the sky so brilliant that "in comparison, the sun seemed dark."

160

Within seconds of the dazzling flash, a devastating explosion rocked the entire area. After it was over, nothing but charred, smoking tree trunks remained.

What had happened?

The first explanation was that it had been a falling meteor of tremendous size. But there was one main fault to this idea. There was no crater left at the point of impact!

Then what?

Today many scientists believe they have the answer to that problem. A fragment from a black hole in its earlier stage of "throwing off" particles may have entered our atmosphere and plunged right through our planet, entering in Siberia and emerging in the North Atlantic. It might have been no larger than a grain of sand, yet weighty enough to pierce our earth's crust, and come out on the other side, continuing its flight through the universe.

Its enormous magnetic powers may have left traces of effect in the Triangle zone, which are still being felt.

There are other universe mind-bogglers, too, like the "earth staggerings."'

Outbursts from the sun vitally affect the weather on earth, which, in turn, can affect the rate of the earth's spin. The bursting energy released by the sun charges our atmosphere, which affects our tides which in turn act with a braking effect on the earth's spin. In such a way, time on earth is affected. A day becomes, from time to time, temporarily shortened.

In August of 1972, on the second day of the month, the sun erupted more violently than it had in decades. Analyzing what had happened in the wake of that explosion, scientists keeping records of such events discovered a leap second or "glitch" in the rate of the earth's spin on August 8th.

The earth does not present a smooth, long-term slowdown, however. Its record is a wobbly graph. Sometimes it shows speed-ups instead of deceleration. These variations may have some bearing on Triangle troubles. In any case, the cosmos itself must be watched if we wish to examine every possible clue in the great Triangle mystery.

# Chapter 20

## IS MAN'S MIND THE KEY?

In the puzzling reports of Triangle mysteries one main factor is recurrent: the confusion and disorientation in the minds of the captains, pilots or radiomen who were involved.

In the well-known instance of the Lost Flight 19, the squadron of five Avenger bombers that took off on December 5th, 1945, from Fort Lauderdale Naval Air Station and disappeared forever in the distance (a case I covered in detail in my *Bermuda Triangle* book), one outstanding conclusion was reached by the investigative board which stated in article 44 of its final report:

"That the disappearance of the squadron planes . . . was caused by a temporary mental confusion resulting in faulty judgment on the part of Flight Leader L. Taylor, permitting himself to lose knowledge of his general position . . . and the facilities available to him in his flight for orienting himself."

This is most strange when all evidence proved later that Taylor was precisely where he should have been, north of the Bahamas!—a fact he didn't know even though he was very familiar with the area, having flown it innumerable times the previous year while he was stationed at Key West. He was also well acquainted with the Avenger plane, having flown it many times before. As for his flying experience, he'd had heavy combat duty in a dive bomber attached to an aircraft carrier in the Pacific. Yet, in this familiar area, he was as though far out at sea, lost and bewildered!

Lieutenant Taylor was not the only pilot to suffer disorientation.

On April of 1962, the control tower at Nassau in the Bahamas picked up a panicky call from a twin-engined Apache. It was coming in on the field from the direction of Great Abaco Island. What astonished the tower personnel was the unbelievable confusion of the pilot as to his position. He communicated as though he were flying in a shroud of inpenetrable fog, when actually the day was as clear as anyone could ask for!

Repeatedly he requested direction, completely unable to ascertain his own position. After many stressed messages, radio contact was cut off. The tower never heard from the pilot again. Obviously, the plane's compass and other instruments were not operating properly. But, being in sight of Nassau as he had to be at the moments of radio contact, why could he not have *seen* where he was and been able to make a safe landing? What confused him? He was disoriented. Why?

Here is one simple example of how disorientation can occur. You can try the experiment yourself, if you can find a frog or a toad. Hold the creature between the palms of your hands; then turn your hands so that the animal is upside down. Now you can remove your upper hand and the toad will remain uncovered on one palm, immobile. He cannot stir because he is disoriented.

So it is with man when he is faced with compasses gone haywire, directional finders that aren't operating, clocks that don't work, etc. He doesn't know where he is, how high he is, or even how long he has been there! He is mentally befuddled and, like the toad upside down, can't function properly. He is completely disoriented.

Disorientation opens the door to what parapsychologists in the study of paranormal phenomena call an "altered state of consciousness." Man's conscious mind becomes subdued, and other levels of thought take over. This altered condition can be brought on by any process that "puts away" the conscious segment of mind. It occurs most frequently when a person goes to sleep. Then the subconscious becomes dominant through dreams. This same dominance comes about when the conscious mind is subdued by hypnosis, drugs, meditation, or trance (a method used frequently by mediums as a pathway for super-psychic sensitivity).

It is in a state of disorientation that the supernormal or psychic experience most often occurs. People who report "astral travel" (that is, leaving their physical bodies, traveling elsewhere—anywhere else in the world—and returning) do so after their conscious minds have been lulled "asleep" in some way.

The same is true for the psychic experience called "teleportation" when a physical object is moved from one place to another by no physical process but by the power of mind alone—an ability dubbed "psychokinesis" by the parapsychologist, meaning the power of "mind over matter."

A Russian medium named Nina Kulagina is one of the most skillful practitioners of psychokinetic powers living in the world today. Her mental feats—moving a glass, cigarettes, and several other objects on a table before her—were photographed on television not so long ago.

Psychokinesis expresses itself most remarkably in a phenomenon called "materialization" or conversely, "dematerialization." An object is "dematerialized" from one spot or area and "re-materialized" in another. Phenomena experienced by residents in a house called "haunted" or "devil-possessed" usually involve this "vanishing" element. The occupants will complain that a book or a pair of glasses or a piece of jewelry disappears, sometimes to reappear in another room (usually in a ridiculous place like the top back shelf of a little-used closet or in an attic trunk, etc.). Spiritualists refer to this as "poltergeist" presence, a term meaning in German "mischievous spirit." A parapsychologist, however, will explain this as having no relation to a spirit or a devil but as being the result of some person's—or persons'—subconscious thought in a psychokinetically active form.

Albert Einstein once confessed to a fellow scientist that he believed man's mind had the ability to dissassemble molecules of matter—and reassemble them, voluntarily or involuntarily.

This process, it would seem, is precisely what happens in dematerialization.

Way-out as this whole theory sounds, it does not seem so implausible when one stops to consider what matter *is*. The Science Museum in London once illustrated matter's substance very clearly. One could see a material object enormously magnified. A piece of lead from a pencil appeared as large and solid as a curbstone in the first instance. In the next magnification it was enlarged again and appeared to be a loosely-woven segment of a wicker basket. In the subsequent magnification, this same strip of lead was so tremendously enlarged we find we are looking at nothing but several strands spread around like a few pieces of hair. The final enlargement brought to view nothing but a scattering of dots scarcely visible!

As Arthur Ford, the renowned medium, once said, "The heaviest brick is mostly empty space!" And so, too, according to this reason, is the biggest aircraft, the stoutest yacht, the heaviest freighter (see Chapter 1!).

Is the key to the Triangle puzzle, then, in man's own mind? The framework of the Triangle puzzle certainly seems to present the perfect setup for a positive answer.

Some force seems to be at work in this area that is related to magnetism. Perhaps it is some electromagnetic force that is propelled from outer space when there is a cosmic disturbance. As the magnetic attraction at the extremities of earth's axis draws toward them the charged particles borne to our planet by a solar wind (a beautiful process that gives us the magnificent displays of the Northern and Southern lights), so perhaps does some super-magnetic pull in the Triangle zone draw an electromagnetic force toward it when a cosmic disturbance has triggered it off.

Such a force would affect the instruments of any craft near it. The malfunctioning instruments would, in turn, affect man's mind, sending it into an altered state—a state of thinking which produces the paranormal or supernormal. In such a condition, he could pass into a dematerialization process—a teleportation—even, perhaps, go so far as to cause himself to supersede mortals' concepts of time!

What is time? Merely man's own bookkeeping method. No such thing as time exists in the universe. Time, as Einstein taught us, is relative. It relates to space and is interlocked with it. The faster one travels out into the universe, the slower time moves. The astronauts out in space are aging more gradually than we are. Time for them has slowed up.

Are men who slip into altered states of consciousness also traveling out of range of our concepts—our limitations of time and space?

Much evidence supports such a theory. One such possible experience may be at the core of the following story which appeared in Bermuda's *Royal Gazette* newspaper on May 20th, 1971. It concerns a British airliner that was flying from New York to Bermuda with fifteen passengers aboard.

Suddenly, as the captain described later, the aircraft started to rise and fall. He wasn't afraid, because he knew the craft was of stout construction and that he had plenty of fuel, but what did bother him was the malfunctioning of his instruments. He was completely incapable of determining his location. For over a half-hour, he had no idea where he was.

He reasoned that he had three alternatives: he

could make a 180-degree turn and return to the U.S.; he could swing to the right and hope to reach Bermuda; or he could push straight ahead and hope to make contact with a radio ship anchored in the Atlantic Ocean.

The captain decided to ask the passengers what their wish in the matter would be. They voted unanimously to continue going straight ahead and hope to make contact with the radio vessel. Fortunately, the captain was able to do just that. His position was given him, and he was able to land safely in Bermuda.

But the strangest part of all was the *time* at which he arrived. He was impossibly far ahead of schedule. It was all a mystery he hasn't solved to this day.

Is the answer related to a "time warp?" Did an electromagnetic atmospheric disturbance cause him and all aboard to move the craft mentally through and out of the usual concepts of time and space?

Many people experience "going back in time," or "going forward in time." One woman came to me a few years ago troubled with a particularly strange psychic experience. Although she was used to much paranormal activity in her life such as telepathy (tuning in to other people's thoughts), she had never had anything like the following occur to her.

She stepped out of John Wanamaker's department store in Philadelphia and was stunned to find herself, not on Market Street as it looks today, but on a strange street as it must have been in the late 1800s! Horse-drawn carriages were rattling by. Vendors were selling their wares. The shops along the avenue were sporting oldtime signs. Children skipped by in long skirts with ribbons bouncing from their curls.

Women were gowned in tight-waisted long skirts. Men pushed by in narrow suits and dark derbies.

Frightened, the woman swung on her heel and hurried back into the store. She closed her eyes, stood quietly off to one side, and waited for her breathing to return to normal.

After a few moments she walked slowly outside again. All was the usual hustle and bustle of today's Market Street. She sighed, relieved, and went on about her business. But she never forgot that strange moment when she stepped back in time.

Do men in the Triangle zones experience much the same thing? In an altered state of consciousness do they, too, slip out of an earth-created concept of time into another dimension—either forward or backward, disassembling all molecules of matter around them as they do so?

For all our deep searching into the mysteries of our universe, do we tend to look too far *outward* into the world around us when our gazing should be *inward*, straight into man's own mind?

Or is the Bermuda Triangle puzzle showing us both directions are the same thing—the universe and its mysteries and man's consciousness and its mysteries are one and the same?

Looking inward to thought, are we also looking outward at the universe?

# Epilogue

## THE LONE SURVIVOR

What puts a survivor—especially a lone survivor—in a class of meritorious distinction? He certainly is unique. From the moment of his rescue, the rest of humanity looks upon him with unabashed curiosity, admiration, and even a little envy.

Possibly the distinction lies in the fact that survival is an outward measure of a man's inner fiber. The well-known Great Lakes historian, William Ratigan, declared some years ago that "There is a magnificence in a man's will to survive . . ."

Most expert seamen feel that the all-important ingredient necessary for survival is not, as most of us would suppose, expert swimming ability but an indomitable will to live.

The Devil's Triangle has been a testing ground for many a person's "will to live."

One such man is a personal acquaintance of mine. His trip into the Triangle started out as a leisurely cruise with friends. It ended in stark tragedy. Without warning and with no apparent cause, the boat began to fill with water. It sank off Cape Hatteras, losing to the sea all the passengers but one.

The man clung to a broken segment of the cabin roof.

Three days later, a New York-bound freighter from Central America noticed him bobbing alone on a piece of wreckage about 60 miles northeast of Cape Hatteras and rescued him.

The trauma is still very real to this day, and he rarely mentions the subject of his sole survival. "It's something I want to forget," he told me.

But the world does not forget the survivor. He represents a phenomenon that his fellow men like to ponder, analyze, and comment upon.

Captain Marryat, an English seaman of the last century who wrote several books about ships and the sea, detailed in one volume a personal point about survival:

"I have witnessed so many miraculous escapes, so many sudden reverses, so much, beyond all hope and conception, achieved by a reliance upon Providence, and under your own exertions, that under the most critical circumstances, I never should despair. If struggling in the center of the Atlantic, with no vessel in sight, no strength remaining, and shaking under the wave that boiled in my ear, as memory and life were departing—still, as long as life did remain, as long as recollection held her seat, I never should abandon Hope—never believe that it is all over with me—till I awoke in the next world, and found it confirmed."

I would like to think of this book as a tribute to those Captains Courageous who persevered through the worst of the Devil's Triangle trials—and won their return.

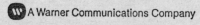

# Your Own Full-Color Map Of The Bermuda Triangle Only $2.95

For a limited time Warner Books is offering a dramatic 18" x 24" full-color map of the sinister body of water where numerous ships and planes have vanished without a trace. Printed on high-quality coated stock, suitable for framing, this handsome poster includes a chronological index of the craft lost in THE BERMUDA TRIANGLE over the centuries and indicates their approximate positions when they disappeared.

## ACT TODAY! SUPPLY IS LIMITED!

To order your copy(ies) of this unique poster, shipped in a protective mailing tube, send this order form together with your check or money order for $2.95 per poster immediately to:

---

**WARNER BOOKS,** P.O. Box 690, New York, N.Y. 10019

Please send me . . . . copy(ies) of THE BERMUDA TRIANGLE POSTER. I have enclosed $ . . . . . . check . . . . . or money order . . . . . as payment in full. No C.O.D.s.

Name . . . . . . . . . . . . . . . . . . . . . . . . . . . . . . . .

Address . . . . . . . . . . . . . . . . . . . . . . . . . . . . . .

City . . . . . . . . . . . . State . . . . . . . . Zip . . . . . .